CHOCOLATE
COOKERY

CHOCOLATE COOKERY

Cathy Gill

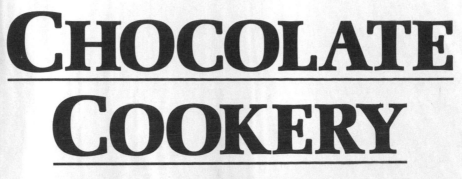

CONTENTS

First published in 1984 by Octopus Books Limited
59 Grosvenor Street, London W1

© Hennerwood Publications Limited

ISBN 0 86273 132 1

Produced by Mandarin Publishers Ltd
22a Westlands Road
Quarry Bay
Hong Kong

Printed in Hong Kong

INTRODUCTION

Smooth, luscious chocolate, one of the world's great luxuries, can be used to create a great variety of delights. In this book we cover the whole field of chocolate thrills, from impressive party-pieces like Profiteroles to children's treats like chocolate toffee and fudge.

Sweet and Simple gives a selection of delicious, easily-made puddings and desserts – chocolate treats you can whip up in a trice to impress family and friends alike. Try the eye-catching Fruit Split, or the Chocolate Soufflé Omelette, made in a moment.

Desserts leads on to the more exotic and impressive chocolate desserts – cheesecakes, pies, trifles and ice creams that would make a grand finale to any dinner party. Impress your guests with Soufflé Monte Carlo or Gingered Charlotte Russe. Thrill them with the elegance of Chocolate Hearts, or spoil them with the classic Profiteroles with Chocolate Sauce.

Gâteaux No chocolate book would be complete without chocolate gâteaux – the chocaholic's delight. Take your pick from 16 wonderful cakes, with a whole medley of shapes, sizes and flavours. For a really grand occasion, try the stunning Meringue Basket, or the Valentine Gâteau, decorated with fresh strawberries.

Party Time is a fun chapter. Here is a whole selection of teatime and party treats, for children and grownups alike. Try the mouthwatering Chocolate Fudge Bars or the Chocolate Finger Dips. And for that special birthday tea, when the cake *must* impress, make one of the spectacular children's fantasy cakes – Ozzy Owl or Thomas Toad will make any birthday memorable!

Round the World shows us that most countries can produce their chocolate treat. We include old favourites such as Bûche de Noel and Devil's Food Cake, as well as some more unusual recipes such as Viennese Chocolate Whirls. We also show that classic cakes can be adapted to make the most of chocolate – even the great Pavlova can be enhanced by the addition of chocolate!

Plain Chocolate
Plain eating chocolate has a rich deep chocolate flavour and is the kind of chocolate most suited to the desserts and cake recipes in this book. It is also suitable for making chocolate decorations and designs. Some of the French-made plain chocolate bars available in supermarkets and delicatessens are specifically produced for desserts and baking. These are less sweet than eating chocolate and give a fine rich flavour for cakes, desserts and confectionery.

Bitter Chocolate
Bitter chocolate is available in some delicatessens and may replace a proportion of the chocolate used in some recipes for a stronger, slightly bitter flavour.

Unsweetened Chocolate
This is difficult to obtain. It is used in American and Canadian cooking and has no substitute. Unsweetened chocolate is not used in this book.

Milk Chocolate
Milk chocolate has a milder chocolate flavour than plain and for this reason is less widely used in cooking. It is made by adding dried milk to the process.

White Chocolate
White chocolate has a higher sugar content than plain chocolate and is usually considered more of a candy than a chocolate. It can be used in cooking, and is included in a few recipes here. Great care should be taken when cooking with white chocolate as it is difficult to melt: it softens very slowly and is apt to become grainy.

Cooking Chocolate
This has a certain amount of the cocoa butter replaced by other fats such as coconut or palm kernel oils. Other flavourings and fillings are also used in the preparation of this chocolate which makes it economical and easy to use. It is suitable for general cake coverings and fillings and can be used for making all chocolate decorations.

Couverture
Couverture chocolate is a rich flavoured chocolate with a high proportion of cocoa butter, giving it a glossy appearance and a smooth texture. To melt and set successfully the chocolate needs to be tempered by repeated heating and cooling. Because it is expensive and difficult to use, it is normally used only by professional confectioners.

Dipping Chocolate
Dipping chocolate, with a high proportion of vegetable fats, is a less expensive alternative to couverture. It has a good flavour and quality and is available in milk or plain.

Chocolate Squares, Triangles and Wedges

Melt 100 g (4 oz) cooking, plain or bitter chocolate, broken into pieces, in a heatproof bowl set over a pan of hot water. Using a flexible palette knife, spread the chocolate 3 mm (⅛ inch) thick on to waxed or non-stick silicone paper, or foil. Leave to set. When set, trim the edges of the chocolate, then use a ruler to mark out even-sized squares or rectangles. Cut out the shapes with a sharp knife. Cut the squares diagonally to make triangles, and cut the rectangles diagonally to make wedges.

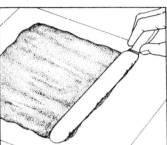

Spread the chocolate evenly on to waxed paper or foil, using a palette knife.

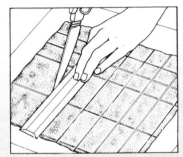

Use a ruler and a sharp knife, to mark out even-sized squares or rectangles.

Melting Chocolate

To melt chocolate successfully, place the chocolate, broken into pieces, in the top of a double boiler or in a small heatproof bowl that will fit securely over the top of a saucepan. Partially fill the pan with hot water, making sure that the water does not touch the bowl or the top of the double boiler. Overheated chocolate becomes stiff and granular. Bring the water almost to the boil, then remove from the heat and place the bowl or top of the double boiler over the pan. Stir with a wooden spoon until melted and smooth.

Chocolate can only be melted in a saucepan when a high proportion of liquid is added at the beginning, for example when making some sauces. The minimum amount of liquid should be 150 ml (¼ pint) and the sauce should be stirred vigorously while melting.

Chocolate Leaves

Melt 50 g (2 oz) cooking, plain or bitter chocolate in a wide heatproof bowl set over a pan of hot water. Stir until smooth, then cool to 36-43°C, 92-110°F, or until it has a smooth, glossy appearance.

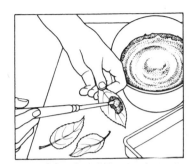

Spread the chocolate over the underside of each leaf, using a fine brush.

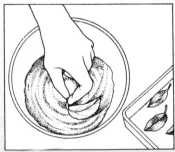

You can also draw the underside of each leaf across the surface of the melted chocolate.

When the leaves are dry, carefully peel away the leaf, starting at the stem.

Chocolate Curls

The chocolate should be at room temperature. Hold the bar of chocolate over a plate and draw the blade of a vegetable peeler along the thin edge of the bar and allow the curls to fall on to the plate.

Grated Chocolate

Chill the chocolate for about 15 minutes then grate it finely or coarsely as desired on to a plate. Hold the

chocolate with a small piece of foil to avoid the fingers melting the chocolate, taking care not to grate the foil as well. Remove the foil as the chocolate gets smaller.

Chopped Chocolate

The chocolate should be at room temperature. Break the chocolate into squares. Place on a chopping board and with a sharp, heavy knife, chop it into pieces.

Chocolate Cut-out Shapes

Melt 100 g (4 oz) cooking, plain or bitter chocolate, broken into pieces, in a heatproof bowl set over a pan of hot water. Using a flexible palette knife, spread the chocolate 3 mm (⅛ inch) thick on to waxed or non-stick silicone paper, or foil. Leave to set. Stamp out shapes using small biscuit cutters. Lift carefully on to a flat plate or board lined with non-stick silicone paper. Avoid handling the shapes as much as possible. The leftover chocolate can be melted and used again.

Chocolate Scrolls

Melt some cooking chocolate, bitter cooking chocolate or plain chocolate as directed on page 7. Using a flexible palette knife, spread the chocolate to a thickness of about 3 mm (⅛ inch) on a cool work surface. Cool until set. Push a long firm knife or metal spatula under the chocolate at a slight angle. Shorter scrolls are formed by pushing the blunt end of a spatula under the chocolate.

Chocolate Caraque

Spread melted chocolate as above and cool until set. Place a sharp, long-bladed knife on the surface of the chocolate and hold the tip of the knife securely. Holding the knife at a slight angle, push the knife slightly into the chocolate and scrape in a quarter circle movement to produce long thin chocolate curls. With practice, very long curls will be made.

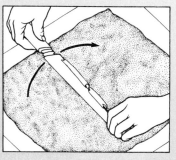

Storing and Chilling Chocolate

Store chocolate in a cool, dry place. During hot weather all chocolate used for decorations may need to be placed in the refrigerator briefly to allow it to set. Remember if you keep chocolate in the refrigerator or freezer for any length of time to wrap it well, as it absorbs odours very easily. The greyish-white film or 'bloom' that you sometimes see on chocolate is the result of cocoa butter or sugar crystals rising to the surface after exposure to varying temperatures. It does not affect the flavour and disappears on melting.

Piped Decorations

Rosettes Using a plain nozzle, gradually press out the icing, moving the tube around in a circle towards the centre to completely enclose the middle. Finish off quickly to leave a raised point.

Stars Hold the piping bag upright over the cake with the tip of the nozzle just above the surface. Pipe out sufficient icing and quickly pull away.

Shells Use a scroll nozzle. Pressing lightly, move the nozzle away from you a little and then towards you, lifting it slightly.

Scrolls With the nozzle close to the surface make a question mark, beginning with a thick head and gradually releasing the pressure to make a long tail. Make a second scroll on the tail of the first, to form a chain, or reverse it to make double scrolls.

Ropes Using a plain nozzle for ropes and lines.

Ribbons Use the flat serrated ribbon nozzle to make basket designs, ribbons, or edgings.

To make a greaseproof paper bag

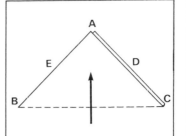

1. Fold a 25 cm (10 inch) square of greaseproof paper in half to form a triangle.

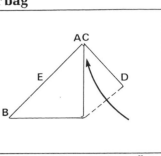

2. Fold point C to point A on a flat surface and crease well.

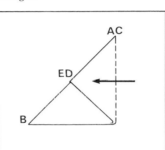

3. Fold point D over to point E and crease well.

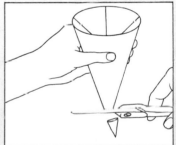

4. Fold point A to point B and crease well.

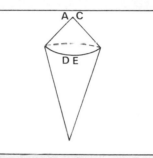

5. Hold the bag where points D and E meet. Shape into a cone, overlap points twice and crease to secure.

6. Cut off the tip of the cone. Do not fill more than half full.

Piping Cream

Use double or whipping cream for piping. The consistency should be soft, so that the cream holds its shape after whipping. Beware of over-whipping double cream, or it may become granular.

To pipe cream, use a nylon piping bag, or greaseproof paper cone, fitted with a metal nozzle. See above for how to make a greaseproof paper bag. Use a spatula to fill the bag or cone. Force out the filling by exerting pressure with the fingers and palm of one hand, while guiding the nozzle with the other hand.

Piping may make the cream go buttery, so that the design goes 'frilly' round the edge. If that happens, wash out the piping bag and start again.

SHORT AND SWEET

STRAWBERRY TRIFLE CAKE

Serves 6-8
100 g (4 oz) self-raising flour
50 g (2 oz) cocoa
175 g (6 oz) soft margarine
175 g (6 oz) caster sugar
3 eggs
butter, for greasing
4 tablespoons medium sherry
4 tablespoons strawberry jam
150 ml (¼ pint) whipping cream
50 g (2 oz) small ratafia biscuits
a few strawberries, to decorate

Preparation time: 15 minutes, plus cooling
Cooking time: 1 hour
Oven: 180°C, 350°F, Gas Mark 4

1. Sift the flour and cocoa into a mixing bowl, then add the margarine, sugar and eggs. Beat with a wooden spoon until thoroughly blended.
2. Spread the mixture evenly in a greased 18 cm (7 inch) deep cake tin. Bake in a preheated oven for about 1 hour until well risen and springy to the touch. Turn the cake out on to a wire tray and cool.
3. Place the cake, still on the wire tray, over a large plate and prick all over with a fine skewer.
4. Spoon 3 tablespoons of the sherry over the cake, then spread the jam on top.
5. Whip the cream. Fold the remaining sherry into the cream and spread over the jam. F
6. Place the ratafias in concentric circles over the cream and decorate with sliced strawberries.

F Thaw at room temperature for 3 hours, then decorate.

Variation
Vary the flavour of the jam according to taste. The trifle cake is equally delicious made with raspberry or black cherry jam.

FRUIT SPLIT

75 g (3 oz) plain chocolate, broken into pieces
25 g (1 oz) butter
1 egg, separated
4 small bananas, peeled and cut lengthways
juice of 1 lemon
2 fresh or canned pineapple rings, roughly chopped
2 kiwi fruit, peeled and sliced
8 lychees, peeled and stoned
8 black grapes, halved and seeded
4 scoops Chocolate fudge ice cream (page 13), (optional)
25 g (1 oz) pine kernels

Preparation time: 20 minutes
Cooking time: 7-8 minutes

Vary the fruits in this dessert with those in season. Sliced strawberries and peaches make a particularly colourful and delicious combination.

1. Place the chocolate and butter in a small heatproof bowl and stand over a pan of hot water until melted. Stir vigorously until smooth.
2. Stir in the egg yolk, then carefully fold in the stiffly beaten egg white.
3. Toss the bananas in the lemon juice and place 2 lengths, rounded side up, on each 'banana split' dish or individual serving plate.
4. Arrange the prepared fruits between the banana lengths and place a scoop of ice cream on top, if using.
5. Drizzle a little chocolate sauce over the banana and ice cream. Sprinkle with the pine kernels and serve immediately, handing the remainder of the sauce separately.

RIGHT: Strawberry trifle cake; Fruit split

PEACH AND CARAMEL GLORY

100 g (4 oz) sugar
4 tablespoons water
150 ml (¼ pint) single cream
1 tablespoon cocoa
4 large ripe peaches or 8 canned peach halves
½ quantity Brown bread and chocolate chip ice cream
  (page 00)
To decorate:
65 ml (2½ fl oz) whipping cream
25 g (1 oz) chopped nuts, toasted
4 glacé cherries
4 Chocolate wedges (page 7)

Preparation time: 15 minutes
Cooking time: about 10 minutes

1. Heat the sugar and water in a small saucepan until the sugar has dissolved. Bring to the boil and continue boiling without stirring, until it is a deep golden caramel.
2. Meanwhile, blend the cream and cocoa in a separate pan and bring to the boil. Standing well back, tip the boiled cream into the caramel. Stir vigorously, and heat gently if necessary to dissolve the caramel. Cool.
3. Place the peaches in a heatproof bowl and cover with boiling water. Leave for 1 minute, then plunge the peaches into cold water to prevent cooking. Peel off the skin, then halve and stone the peaches. Cut the halves into quarters.
4. Put alternate layers of peach quarters and scoops of ice cream in 4 tall sundae glasses. Finish with a scoop of ice cream.
5. Whip the cream. To decorate, pour the caramel sauce over each dessert. Decorate with a large rosette of whipped cream, sprinkle with the nuts and top with a cherry. Insert a chocolate wedge beside each cherry. Serve immediately. If necessary, they will hold for 15 minutes in the refrigerator before serving.

RIGHT: Peach and caramel glory; Pineapple with coconut sauce

PINEAPPLE WITH COCONUT SAUCE

1 medium pineapple, peeled, cored and sliced into 8 rings
1 tablespoon clear honey
juice of 1 lemon
2 tablespoons white rum
25 g (1 oz) butter
Coconut sauce:
2 tablespoons cocoa
3 tablespoons clear honey
150 ml (¼ pint) water
1 tablespoon white rum
50 g (2 oz) creamed coconut
2 tablespoons single cream
25 g (1 oz) shredded or desiccated coconut, toasted
   (optional)

Preparation time: 15 minutes, plus standing overnight
Cooking time: 10 minutes

1. Place the pineapple rings in a large shallow dish. Combine the honey, lemon juice and rum and pour over the pineapple. Cover, and chill overnight.
2. Drain the pineapple rings and reserve the marinade. Heat the butter in a large pan and lightly fry the pineapple rings without letting them colour. Transfer to a heated serving dish and keep warm.
3. To make the sauce, blend the reserved marinade, cocoa, honey, water and rum. Heat gently, then add the creamed coconut and cream, a little at a time. Stir until completely melted.
4. Arrange 2 slices of pineapple on each plate, pour some sauce over the top and sprinkle with coconut.

CHOCOLATE FUDGE ICE CREAM

Serves 6-8
4 egg yolks
1 tablespoon cocoa
150 ml (¼ pint) water
100 g (4 oz) soft brown sugar
450 ml (¾ pint) double cream
Fudge:
25 g (1 oz) butter
50 g (2 oz) plain chocolate, broken into pieces
1 tablespoon milk
100 g (4 oz) icing sugar, sieved
25 g (1 oz) almonds, chopped and toasted

Preparation time: about 25 minutes, plus freezing

1. Turn the freezer to the fast freeze setting, or the refrigerator to its coldest setting. Beat the egg yolks and cocoa together until thick and creamy.

BROWN BREAD AND CHOCOLATE CHIP ICE CREAM

Serves 6-8
600 ml (1 pint) double cream
1 tablespoon caster sugar
100 g (4 oz) fresh brown breadcrumbs
75 g (3 oz) soft dark brown sugar
50 g (2 oz) hazelnuts, chopped and toasted
100 g (4 oz) bitter dessert or plain chocolate, roughly
   chopped

Preparation time: about 20 minutes, plus freezing

1. Turn the freezer to the fast freeze setting, or the refrigerator to its coldest setting.
2. Whip the cream with the caster sugar until it holds its shape on the whisk. Transfer to a freezer tray or lidded container so that it can be beaten easily.
3. Freeze the cream for 30 minutes, beat thoroughly, then freeze again for a further 30 minutes.
4. Meanwhile, spread the breadcrumbs on the grill pan and sprinkle the sugar over the top. Place under a preheated grill until the sugar caramelizes. Stir well to ensure even browning. Cool.
5. If necessary, grind or crush the breadcrumbs to break down any lumps. Stir in the hazelnuts.
6. Remove the frozen cream from the freezer and beat thoroughly. Stir in the breadcrumb mixture and lastly the chopped chocolate. Mix well, then return to the freezer for a further 2 hours.
7. If the ice cream has been frozen for 24 hours or longer, remove from the freezer and allow to soften for 1 hour before serving.

2. Place the water and sugar in a small saucepan and heat gently until the sugar dissolves. Boil rapidly for 5 minutes. Remove from the heat.
3. Pour the syrup in a steady stream on to the yolks, beating constantly. Continue beating until cool. The mixture should be very light and creamy.
4. Whisk the cream until it holds its shape on the whisk, then fold into the egg yolk mixture. Transfer the mixture to a freezing tray and place in the freezer for 1½ hours. Beat thoroughly every 30 minutes.
5. Meanwhile, place the butter, chocolate and milk in a heatproof bowl and stand over a pan of hot water. Stir until smooth and melted. Pour into the icing sugar and beat to a smooth paste. Refrigerate until set.
6. Roughly chop the fudge and add to the ice cream together with the almonds. Beat thoroughly, and freeze for 30 minutes; remove from the freezer, beat again, then freeze for a further 30 minutes. If the ice cream has been frozen for 24 hours or longer, soften in the refrigerator for 15 minutes before serving.

PEARS WITH MAPLE SYRUP SAUCE

4 large ripe pears, peeled, stalks removed
75 g (3 oz) chocolate cake crumbs
25 g (1 oz) walnuts, chopped
3 maraschino cherries, chopped
1-2 tablespoons maraschino cherry syrup
butter, for greasing
8 tablespoons maple syrup
3 teaspoons cocoa
chocolate leaves, to decorate (optional)

Preparation time: 20 minutes
Cooking time: about 25-30 minutes
Oven: 180°C, 350°F, Gas Mark 4

1. Cut a slice from the rounded end of the pears so that they will stand upright.
2. Slice off about 2.5 cm (1 inch) of the pear at the stalk end to form a lid, then scoop out the core with a teaspoon.
3. Combine the cake crumbs, walnuts, cherries and maraschino syrup in a small bowl and mix to a stiff paste. Spoon the mixture neatly into the cavities of the pears. Replace the lids.
4. Place the pears on a lightly greased ovenproof serving dish and cook in a preheated oven for 25-30 minutes until tender. The cooking time will depend on the ripeness of the pear. Test by inserting a fine skewer into the widest part of the pear.
5. Meanwhile, make the sauce by blending the syrup with the cocoa in a small saucepan. Heat until boiling, stirring constantly. Pour into the serving dish to surround the pears, or pour a little into individual serving dishes and carefully place a pear in each one. Decorate with chocolate leaves, if liked.

LEMON SILK CRUNCH

grated rind and juice of 2 lemons
1 teaspoon powdered gelatine
4 tablespoons caster sugar
300 ml (½ pint) double or whipping cream, whipped
100 g (4 oz) chocolate digestive biscuits, finely crushed
50 g (2 oz) almonds, chopped and toasted
Chocolate scrolls (page 8) to decorate

Preparation time: 15 minutes, plus cooling and setting

1. Strain the lemon juice into a cup and sprinkle the gelatine over the juice.
2. Stand the cup in a small pan containing a little hot water. Heat until the gelatine has dissolved. Cool until just beginning to thicken.
3. Fold the gelatine mixture, sugar and lemon rind into the whipped cream until evenly blended. Chill until set, about 2 hours.
4. Combine the biscuits and almonds. Spoon alternate layers of biscuit mixture and lemon mixture into 4 individual glasses, ending with a layer of lemon.
5. Just before serving, decorate each glass with Chocolate scrolls.

LEFT TO RIGHT: Pears with maple syrup sauce; Chocolate muesli delight; Lemon silk crunch

CHOCOLATE MUESLI DELIGHT

1 × 450 g (16 oz) carton thick set plain unsweetened yogurt
50 g (2 oz) unsweetened muesli base
50 g (2 oz) hazelnuts, finely chopped and toasted
225 g (8 oz) dried apricots
2 tablespoons clear honey
100 g (4 oz) plain chocolate
25 g (1 oz) butter
Chocolate curls (page 7), to decorate

Preparation time: 20 minutes

1. Tip the yogurt into a mixing bowl and stir in the muesli base and hazelnuts.

2. Roughly chop the apricots, then stir the chopped apricots and honey into the yogurt mixture until evenly blended.

3. Melt the chocolate with the butter in a small heat-proof bowl set over hot water. Stir vigorously until smooth.

4. Spoon one tablespoon of the yogurt mixture into the bottom of 4 tall glass sundae goblets. On top, spoon 2 teaspoons of the chocolate mixture, swirling the mixture against the side of the glass, without stirring it into the yogurt.

5. Continue spooning the yogurt and chocolate alternately into the glasses until a rippled effect is achieved. Spoon any leftover chocolate on top. Ⓐ

6. Decorate the deserts with Chocolate scrolls. Serve immediately or serve chilled.

Ⓐ Can be made a day in advance and kept chilled. Decorate just before serving.

CHOCOLATE BANANA PIE

Serves 4-6

175 g (6 oz) chocolate digestive biscuits, finely crushed
50 g (2 oz) butter, melted
2 small bananas
1 × 383 g (13½ oz) can condensed milk
grated rind and juice of 1 lemon
2 teaspoons powdered gelatine
100 g (4 oz) plain chocolate, broken into pieces
25 g (1 oz) butter
To decorate: (optional)
1 small banana
a little lemon juice

**Preparation time: 15 minutes,
plus setting and chilling**

LEFT TO RIGHT: Chocolate banana pie; Raspberry and lychee crisp; Chocolate syllabub

This pie is best eaten on the day it is made, as the banana filling will discolour and the topping will soften if refrigerated overnight.

1. Mix the biscuit crumbs with the melted butter, then press on to the base of a 20 cm (8 inch) fluted porcelain pie dish or metal flan tin.
2. Purée the bananas with two-thirds of the condensed milk. Pour into a mixing bowl and add the lemon rind.
3. Strain the lemon juice into a cup and sprinkle the gelatine on top. Stand the cup in a small pan containing a little hot water. Heat until the gelatine has dissolved, stirring continually. Stir into the banana mixture and pour the filling into the pie dish. Leave in a cool place to set for about 1 hour.
4. Combine the remaining condensed milk, chocolate and butter and stand in a heatproof bowl over a pan of hot water. Heat gently and stir until thoroughly blended. Cool slightly, then pour over the banana filling and smooth evenly. Chill for at least 2 hours and up to 6 hours.
5. If liked, decorate with sliced banana tossed in a little lemon juice just before serving.

CHOCOLATE SYLLABUB

4 tablespoons drinking chocolate powder
50 ml (2 fl oz) sweet sherry
1 tablespoon brandy
300 ml (½ pint) double cream
2 egg whites
100 g (4 oz) plain chocolate, grated

Preparation time: 10 minutes

1. Blend 3 tablespoons of the drinking chocolate with the sherry and brandy until smooth.
2. In a separate bowl, whip the cream until it just holds its shape on the whisk, then gradually fold the chocolate liquid into the cream.
3. Whisk the egg whites until they stand in soft peaks, then carefully fold these into the cream mixture together with the grated chocolate.
4. Spoon the mixture into 4 very tall individual stemmed glasses. Serve immediately or stand in a cool place for up to 6 hours. Do not refrigerate.
5. Just before serving, sprinkle the surface of each syllabub with a little of the remaining drinking chocolate. Serve with langues de chat biscuits.

STUFFED PEACHES

Serves 4-6
1 × 825 g (1 lb 11 oz) can peach halves, drained
butter, for greasing
50 g (2 oz) ground almonds
2 teaspoons soft brown sugar
15 g (½ oz) butter, softened
1 egg yolk
Sauce:
75 g (3 oz) plain chocolate, broken into pieces
150 ml (¼ pint) single cream
25 g (1 oz) butter
1 egg yolk
2 tablespoons brandy
50 g (2 oz) flaked almonds, toasted

Preparation time: 20 minutes
Cooking time: 15 minutes
Oven: 150°C, 300°F, Gas Mark 2

The number and size of peach halves in a tin can vary, but as a guide, only 1-2 halves should be chopped for the filling.

RASPBERRY AND LYCHEE CRISP

50 g (2 oz) butter
100 g (4 oz) coarse brown breadcrumbs
2 tablespoons brown sugar
1 teaspoon ground cinnamon
grated rind of 1 orange
100 g (4 oz) plain chocolate, grated
350 g (12 oz) fresh raspberries
1 × 310 g (11 oz) can lychees, drained and roughly chopped

Preparation time: 15 minutes, plus cooling

1. Melt the butter in a large frying pan or saucepan. Fry the breadcrumbs until they are crisp and golden brown and all the butter has been absorbed.
2. Transfer to a bowl and cool slightly. Ⓐ Stir in the sugar, cinnamon, rind and half the grated chocolate and mix thoroughly.
3. Reserving 12 raspberries for decoration, place alternate layers of the breadcrumb mixture and the raspberries and lychees in a 600 ml (1 pint) glass serving dish. Top the last layer with a thick covering of the remaining chocolate and decorate with clusters of the reserved raspberries. Ⓐ

Ⓐ The breadcrumb mixture can be made a day in advance. Store in an airtight container. When the whole dessert is made in advance, refrigerate until ready to serve.

1. Dry the peaches thoroughly on paper towels. Place 4 halves in a lightly greased ovenproof dish. Reserve 4 more halves and chop the remainder.
2. Combine the almonds, sugar, butter, egg yolk and chopped peaches and beat to a smooth paste. Spoon the mixture into the cavities of the peaches in the serving dish.
3. Top each stuffed peach with a reserved peach half to form a whole fruit. Bake in a preheated oven for about 15 minutes, until the filling is warmed through.
4. Place the chocolate and cream in a small saucepan. Heat gently without boiling until the chocolate has melted. Stir vigorously until well blended.
5. Cool slightly, then add the butter, egg yolk and brandy.
6. Using 2 spoons, carefully lift the peaches into individual serving dishes and coat with the sauce. Sprinkle with the toasted almonds, and serve warm.

Variation:
To serve chilled, allow the peaches to cool in the ovenproof dish, then transfer to individual serving dishes. Chill for 3-4 hours before serving. Chill the sauce separately.

PANCAKES WITH RUM AND RAISIN SAUCE

Serves 4-6
75 g (3 oz) plain flour
25 g (1 oz) drinking chocolate powder
1 egg
300 ml (½ pint) milk
vegetable oil, for frying
Sauce:
75 g (3 oz) plain chocolate, broken into pieces
150 ml (¼ pint) single cream
2 tablespoons rum
50 g (2 oz) raisins
caster sugar, for sprinkling

Preparation time: 5 minutes
Cooking time: 30 minutes

1. Sieve the flour and drinking chocolate into a mixing bowl.
2. Make a well in the centre and add the egg. Add a little milk, then stir with a wooden spoon, gradually incorporating the flour to make a thick paste. Slowly add half the milk, mixing well between each addition. Pour in the remaining milk. Alternatively, place all the batter ingredients in an electric blender and blend for 10 seconds.
3. Add sufficient oil to put a thin coat on the base of a 15 cm (6 inch) shallow frying pan or crêpe pan. The pan should be very hot before the batter is poured in.
4. Pour in enough batter to cover the base thinly, tilting the pan to spread it evenly.
5. Cook the pancake for about 1 minute, until the underside has browned, then flip the pancake over with a palette knife. Cook the second side for a further minute.
6. Turn the pancake on to a plate, then fold in half and half again to form a wedge. Ⓐ Place on a serving dish and keep warm. Make the rest of the pancakes in the same way, re-oiling the pan each time.
7. To make the sauce, combine the chocolate and cream in a small saucepan. Heat gently, without boiling, until melted, then stir vigorously until smooth. Stir in the rum and raisins. Ⓐ
8. Sprinkle a little caster sugar over the pancakes, then spoon some of the sauce over them. Serve the remainder separately.

Ⓐ The pancakes and sauce can be made the day before. Keep separate, cover and chill. To reheat, place pancakes under a preheated grill until hot and crisp.

Variation:
Make Whisky and walnut sauce by replacing the rum in the sauce with whisky and the raisins with an equal amount of chopped toasted walnuts.

MOCHA DESSERT CUPS

150 g (5 oz) plain chocolate, broken into pieces
50 g (2 oz) butter
50 g (2 oz) caster sugar
150 ml (¼ pint) milk
1 egg (size 1, 2)
1 teaspoon instant coffee powder or granules
50 g (2 oz) ratafia biscuits
1 tablespoon liqueur, e.g. Tia Maria
4 tablespoons double cream

Preparation time: 15 minutes, plus setting
Cooking time: about 10 minutes

This is a simple dessert which can be made in the morning and kept chilled. It is very rich, so serve in small elegant individual dishes accompanied by ratafia biscuits sandwiched together with a little whipped cream, if liked.

1. Melt the chocolate in a small heatproof basin set over a pan of hot water. Stir vigorously until smooth.
2. Cream the butter and sugar together in a mixing bowl until light and fluffy, then stir in the melted chocolate.
3. Beat the milk and egg together thoroughly, then strain into a heavy-based saucepan. Whisk in the instant coffee. Over a gentle heat, stir until the custard thickens sufficiently to coat the back of a wooden spoon. Do not boil.
4. Gradually pour the custard over the chocolate mixture and mix well to blend evenly. Chill until beginning to thicken, about 2 hours.
5. Place the ratafias in a small bowl. Pour on the liqueur and allow to soak into the biscuits.
6. When the chocolate mixture is almost set, spoon half the mixture into 4 glass sundae dishes or wine glasses. Place the ratafias on top of the mixture, then spoon over the remaining chocolate.
7. Swirl one teaspoon of the cream on top of the dessert and chill for at least 2 hours before serving. Serve with ratafias sandwiched together with a little whipped cream, if liked, and arranged attractively on a separate serving dish.

TOP TO BOTTOM: Pancakes with rum and raisin sauce; Chocolate soufflé omelette; Mocha dessert cups

CHOCOLATE SOUFFLÉ OMELETTE

Serves 2

3 tablespoons drinking chocolate powder

2 eggs (sizes 1 or 2), separated

grated rind of ½ orange (optional)

2 tablespoons milk

15 g (½ oz) butter

1 tablespoon orange marmalade, jam or Special chocolate sauce (page 21) to serve, warmed

To decorate:

julienne strips of orange rind or 1 teaspoon grated plain or milk chocolate

Preparation time: 5 minutes

Cooking time: 10 minutes

1. Beat the drinking chocolate, egg yolks, orange rind, if using, and milk together until smooth.

2. Whisk the egg whites until very stiff, then fold into the chocolate mixture.

3. Heat the butter in a 20 cm (8 inch) omelette pan, then carefully pour in the mixture, spreading it evenly with a palette knife.

4. Cook over a moderate heat until the underside is browned, then place the pan with the omelette under a preheated grill for a short time, to brown the top lightly.

5. To serve, pour the marmalade, jam or sauce over half the omelette, then fold the other half over and transfer to a serving dish. Sprinkle with julienne strips of orange rind or grated chocolate and serve immediately.

APRICOT CHOCOLATE FOOL

2 tablespoons custard powder
1 tablespoon cocoa
2 tablespoons drinking chocolate powder
2 tablespoons sugar
300 ml (½ pint) milk
1 × 420 g (14 oz) can apricot halves, drained
300 ml (½ pint) double cream, whipped
1 tablespoon apricot wine or brandy (optional)
Chocolate triangles (page 7)

Preparation time: 15 minutes, plus cooling
Cooking time: 7 minutes

1. Blend the custard powder, cocoa, drinking chocolate powder and sugar with a little of the cold milk.
2. Bring the remaining milk to the boil, then pour over the blended mixture. Stir thoroughly and return to the rinsed pan. Bring to the boil, then cook gently for 2-3 minutes, stirring constantly.
3. Reserve 2 apricots for decoration and purée the remainder with the chocolate custard, then pour into a mixing bowl and cool. Press a piece of cling film on to the surface to prevent a skin forming.
4. When cold, fold in two-thirds of the cream and the wine or brandy, if using, then pour into a serving dish. Ⓐ
5. Decorate with large rosettes of the remaining cream and push a Chocolate triangle into each. Slice the remaining apricots and place a slice beside each triangle.

Ⓐ Can be made a day in advance and kept chilled. Decorate just before serving.

Apricot chocolate fool

QUICK CHOCOLATE SAUCE

Makes about 300 ml (½ pint)
2 tablespoons cocoa
4 tablespoons golden syrup or honey
50 g (2 oz) chilled butter, diced
150 ml (¼ pint) milk
½ teaspoon vanilla essence

Cooking time: 5-7 minutes

1. Blend all the ingredients in a small saucepan. Heat until smooth and melted, stirring constantly.
2. Bring to the boil and cook gently for 2-3 minutes. Use hot or cold.

CHOCOLATE BUTTERSCOTCH SAUCE

Makes about 300 ml (½ pint)
50 g (2 oz) demerara sugar
2 tablespoons drinking chocolate powder
50 g (2 oz) butter
175 ml (6 fl oz)) milk

Cooking time: about 7 minutes

1. Combine the sugar, drinking chocolate and butter in a saucepan and stir over a low heat until the sugar has dissolved.
2. Increase the heat and cook for 2 minutes.
3. Away from the heat, stir in the milk. Bring to the boil and cook for 2 minutes. Use warm or cold.

FUDGE SAUCE

Makes about 300 ml (½ pint)
75 g (3 oz) plain chocolate, broken into pieces
25 g (1 oz) butter
1 × 175 g (6 oz) can evaporated milk
50 g (2 oz) soft brown sugar
¼ teaspoon vanilla essence

Cooking time: about 5 minutes

1. Combine all the ingredients in a saucepan and stir continuously over a low heat until the chocolate has melted and the sugar has dissolved. Do not boil.
2. Serve hot or warm.

Making chocolate sauces
1. When heating ingredients directly in a pan, use a heavy-based pan such as cast iron or aluminium. Thin pans may cause uneven melting or even burning of ingredients.
2. Stir constantly when making sauces to achieve smooth results.
3. Melted chocolate should not be boiled as overheating causes it to become gritty.
4. Cocoa and other sauce ingredients are best heated directly in a saucepan. The grains need partial cooking to eliminate a powdery texture.
5. In the recipes using cocoa, if you wish to achieve a milder chocolate flavour, substitute chocolate drinking powder. Remember to taste for sweetness, as drinking chocolate powder already contains some sugar.
6. Drinking chocolate powder dissolves easily and does not require heating.
7. Malted chocolate drinking powder or granules may be used in place of cocoa for a more unusual flavour.
8. Lumps can be smoothed by liquidizing or whisking the sauce with a small balloon whisk.
9. Most chocolate sauces thicken on cooling and may be thinned by beating in a little milk or liqueur, such as Tia Maria.

SPECIAL CHOCOLATE SAUCE

Makes about 300 ml (½ pint)
100 g (4 oz) plain chocolate, broken into pieces
150 ml (¼ pint) single cream
50 g (2 oz) chilled butter, diced
2 egg yolks
1 tablespoon strong black coffee
1 tablespoon rum

Cooking time: 5-7 minutes

1. Place the chocolate and the cream in a small saucepan and stir over a low heat until the chocolate has melted. Do not boil.
2. Away from the heat, add the butter and stir until melted.
3. Stir in the remaining ingredients and beat until smooth. Use warm or cold.

DESSERTS

SOUFFLÉ MONTE CARLO

4 eggs (size 1 or 2), separated
75 g (3 oz) caster sugar
3 teaspoons instant coffee powder or granules
1 tablespoon hot water
150 ml (¼ pint) water
15 g (½ oz) powdered gelatine
450 ml (¾ pint) double cream, whipped
100 g (4 oz) plain Chocolate caraque (page 8)
100 g (4 oz) ratafia biscuits or 4 large macaroons
   13 cm (5 inches) in diameter, roughly broken
4 tablespoons Tia Maria
To decorate:
8 candied coffee beans

Preparation time: 30 minutes, plus cooling and setting

1. Make a paper collar with a double thickness of greaseproof paper to stand 7.5 cm (3 inches) above the rim of a 15 cm (6 inch) soufflé dish. Secure with string or an elastic band.
2. Beat the egg yolks and sugar until light and creamy. Dissolve the coffee in the hot water and add to the mixture.
3. Pour the 150 ml (¼ pint) water into a small heat-proof bowl and sprinkle over the gelatine. Set the bowl over a pan of water and heat gently, stirring until dissolved. Stir into the mixture and chill until on the point of setting, about 1 hour.
4. Fold two-thirds of the cream into the mixture. Whisk the egg whites until they stand in soft peaks and carefully fold into the coffee mixture.
5. Paint a 450 g (1 lb) jam jar with cooking oil and stand it in the centre of the soufflé dish. Carefully layer the soufflé mixture with three-quarters of the Chocolate caraque around the jar, ending with a layer of soufflé. Smooth level, then chill until set.
6. Place the ratafia biscuits or macaroons in a small bowl and spoon over the Tia Maria. Leave until the liqueur has been soaked up.
7. Carefully pour a little warm water into the jam jar in the centre of the soufflé. Leave for 3-5 seconds then lift out the jar.
8. Spoon the macaroon mixture into the hollow and top with the remaining caraque. Carefully peel away the paper collar.
9. To decorate, pipe rosettes with the remaining cream and finish with candied coffee beans.

HOT LIQUEUR SOUFFLÉ

butter, for greasing
caster sugar, for sprinkling
50 g (2 oz) butter
50 g (2 oz) plain flour
300 ml (½ pint) milk
75 g (3 oz) plain dark or white chocolate, broken into pieces
2 tablespoons Crème de Menthe
3 eggs, separated
1 egg white
50 g (2 oz) caster sugar
Sauce:
150 ml (¼ pint) double cream
50 g (2 oz) plain dark or white chocolate, broken into pieces
2 tablespoons Crème de Menthe
1 egg yolk

Preparation time: 20 minutes
Cooking time: 45 minutes-1 hour
Oven: 180°C, 350°F, Gas Mark 4

1. Butter an 18 cm (7 inch) soufflé dish and dust with the sugar.
2. Combine the butter, flour and milk in a medium saucepan. Stirring continuously, heat gently until boiling. Stir vigorously until a thick paste is formed. Cook for 2-3 minutes, still stirring.
3. Away from the heat, add the chocolate and stir until smooth and completely blended into the sauce.
4. Beat in the liqueur and egg yolks.
5. Whisk the 4 egg whites until very stiff, then add the sugar. Whisk again until very stiff and with a metal spoon fold the chocolate sauce into the egg whites, taking care not to knock the air out of the whites.
6. Pour the soufflé mixture into the prepared soufflé dish and bake in a preheated oven for 45-50 minutes, until well risen. Do not open the oven door during the cooking time or the soufflé with drop.
7. To make the sauce, pour the cream into a small saucepan and add the chocolate. Heat gently, stirring constantly until the chocolate has melted and is thoroughly smooth. Do not boil. Stir in the liqueur and egg yolk. Pour into a jug.
8. To serve, dust the soufflé with icing sugar and take it directly from the oven to a heatproof mat on the table. The soufflé has about 3 minutes after it is taken from the oven. Serve with the sauce.

LEFT: Soufflé Monte Carlo RIGHT: Hot liqueur soufflé

GINGERED CHARLOTTE RUSSE

Serves 6-8
1 teaspoon powdered gelatine
65 ml (2½ fl oz) water
65 ml (2½ fl oz) ginger wine
1 half maraschino cherry
5 crystallized orange or canned mandarin orange segments
1 thin strip angelica, about 5 cm (2 inches) long
about 20 boudoir biscuits
Bavarois:
2 eggs, separated
50 g (2 oz) caster sugar
250 ml (8 fl oz) milk
50 g (2 oz) bitter or plain chocolate, broken into pieces
15 g (½ oz) powdered gelatine
50 ml (2 fl oz) ginger wine
300 ml (½ pint) double cream, whipped
To decorate:
1 metre (1 yard) ribbon

Preparation time: 25 minutes, plus cooling and chilling
Cooking time: 15 minutes

1. Sprinkle the gelatine over the water in a small heatproof bowl. Set the bowl over a pan of hot water and stir until dissolved. Remove from the heat and stir in the ginger wine.
2. Pour in enough gelatine mixture to coat the base of a 15 cm (6 inch) deep, 15 cm (6 inch) diameter cake tin with a fixed base, or similar-sized charlotte mould.
3. Place the cherry half, rounded side down, on the base. Surround with 5 orange segments to represent a flower and use the angelica to form a stalk. Position them at least 1 cm (½ inch) in from the edge to allow room for the biscuits. Chill until set, about 30 minutes. Prevent the remaining gelatine mixture from setting by standing the bowl in a pan of warm water.
4. Carefully pour the remaining gelatine mixture over the set jelly in the tin. Line the sides of the cake tin with the boudoir biscuits, pushing one end into the jelly. Ⓐ
5. To make the Bavarois, beat the yolks and sugar in a bowl until light and creamy. Scald the milk and chocolate in a saucepan (bringing it to just under boiling point) and whisk until smooth, then pour on to the yolk mixture.
6. Return the custard to the rinsed pan and heat gently, without boiling. Stir until the mixture is thick enough to coat the back of a wooden spoon, about 10 minutes. Remove from the heat.
7. Sprinkle the gelatine over the ginger wine in a heatproof bowl. Set the bowl over a pan of hot water and stir until dissolved. Stir into the custard. Cool the custard, then chill until on the point of setting, about 1 hour.

LEFT TO RIGHT: Gingered charlotte russe; Pear upside down pudding; Mandarin yogurt dessert

8. Fold half the cream into the Bavarois mixture, then carefully fold in the stiffly beaten egg whites. Pour into the prepared cake tin and chill until set, about 3 hours.
9. If necessary, trim the tips of the biscuits to the level of the Bavarois filling with a sharp knife. Ⓐ Ⓕ
10. Unmould the charlotte by dipping the base in hot water and turning it out. Decorate with rosettes of the remaining cream and Chocolate triangles, if liked. Carefully tie 1 metre (1 yard) length of ribbon around the Charlotte Russe and finish with a large bow.

Ⓐ Can be prepared the day before and kept chilled.
Ⓕ Thaw in the refrigerator for 6 hours, then unmould and decorate.

PEAR UPSIDE DOWN PUDDING

Serves 6-8
50 g (2 oz) butter
50 g (2 oz) dark brown sugar
1×825 g (1 lb 13 oz) can pear halves, drained
8-10 whole glacé cherries
100 g (4 oz) hard or soft margarine
100 g (4 oz) caster sugar
2 eggs
100 g (4 oz) self-raising flour
25 g (1 oz) cocoa
flaked almonds, to decorate (optional)

Preparation time: 15 minutes
Cooking time: about 35 minutes
Oven: 180°C, 350°F, Gas Mark 4

1. Heat the butter and brown sugar gently until melted, then pour into the base of an 18 cm (7 inch) deep cake tin with a fixed base. Spread evenly over the base.
2. Arrange the pears, rounded side up, on the base of the tin. The number that will fit on the base will depend on the size of the pear halves. Slide a whole glacé cherry into the cavity under each pear. Chop the remaining pears.
3. Cream the fat and sugar until light and fluffy. Beat in the eggs one at a time, then fold in the sieved flour and cocoa.
4. Add the chopped pears to the mixture. Stir well, then carefully spoon over the pears in the tin. Gently smooth over so the mixture is level.
5. Bake in a preheated oven for about 35 minutes, or until the pudding is well risen and springy to the touch. Turn out upside down on to a serving dish. Decorate with flaked almonds, if liked. Serve hot with a pouring custard or single cream.

MANDARIN YOGURT DESSERT

1×300 g (11 oz) can mandarin orange segments, drained, juice reserved
caster sugar, for sweetening
15 g (½ oz) powdered gelatine
100 g (4 oz) plain chocolate
250 ml (8 fl oz) plain unsweetened yogurt
2 tablespoons Curaçao or other orange liqueur (optional)
To decorate: (optional)
50 ml (2 fl oz) whipping cream
orange segment
Chocolate leaf (page 7)

Preparation time: 15 minutes, plus setting

1. Pour the juice from the mandarin oranges into a small saucepan. If the segments were in natural juice, add sugar to taste. Sprinkle the gelatine over the juice and heat gently, without boiling, until dissolved.
2. Break 75 g (3 oz) of the chocolate into pieces and place in a heatproof mixing bowl. Set the bowl over a pan of hot water and heat gently, stirring until melted.
3. Gradually stir in the yogurt, beating vigorously until smooth. Stir in the fruit juice. Reserve 1 orange segment and add the rest, roughly chopped. Grate the remaining chocolate and add to the mixture, together with the liqueur, if using.
4. Pour the mixture into a 600 ml (1 pint) decorative mould and chill until set, about 0 hours.
5. Unmould the pudding and decorate with cream, orange segment and Chocolate leaf, if liked.

BANANA BAVAROIS

½ × 150 g (5 oz) packet lemon jelly
250 ml (8 fl oz) hot water
2 small bananas
Bavarois:
2 eggs, separated
2 tablespoons sugar
grated rind of ½ lemon
½ teaspoon vanilla essence
150 ml (¾ pint) milk
2 teaspoons powdered gelatine
300 ml (½ pint) whipping cream
100 g (4 oz) plain chocolate, broken into pieces

Preparation time: 25 minutes, plus cooling and chilling
Cooking time: 15 minutes

1. Dissolve the jelly in the hot water, then pour in sufficient to cover the base of a 450 g (1 lb) loaf tin. Chill until set.
2. Slice the bananas thinly, discarding the ends and toss in the remaining jelly. Drain, and reserve the jelly. Stand the container with the jelly in a bowl of warm water, to prevent it setting.
3. Position the banana slices, slightly overlapping, in 3-4 rows running the length of the loaf tin. Leave to set, then carefully spoon over the liquid jelly.
4. To make the Bavarois, beat the yolks, sugar, lemon rind and vanilla until light and creamy. Scald the milk, then pour it over the yolk mixture.
5. Return the Bavarois to the rinsed pan and heat gently, without boiling, until the mixture is thick enough to coat the back of a wooden spoon, about 10 minutes. Remove from the heat.
6. Whisking the Bavarois with a fork, gradually sprinkle in the gelatine and stir until dissolved. Cool, then chill until on the point of setting, about 1 hour.
7. Whip the cream, fold in half, then carefully fold in

the stiffly beaten egg whites. Pour into the prepared loaf tin and chill until set, about 3 hours.  Unmould on to a serving dish.

8. Using a palette knife, coat the sides of the Bavarois with a thin layer of the remaining cream.

9. Place the chocolate in a heatproof bowl and set over a pan of hot water. Stir until melted. Draw a rectangle 20×30 cm (8×12 inches) on a piece of greaseproof paper and, using a palette knife, spread the melted chocolate over the rectangle. Leave in a cool place until it is set.

10. Cut the chocolate into rectangles 5×2.5 cm (2× 1 inches)  and place them overlapping (the longest side vertical) all the way around the Bavarois, pressing them gently against the cream. Decorate with rosettes, using the remaining cream.

 The Bavarois can be made a day in advance.
 The chocolate rectangles can be made up to 3 days in advance and stored in a container in a cool place. Decorate the Bavarois the morning before serving.

STEAMED FUDGE PUDDING

25 g (1 oz) butter
1 tablespoon cocoa
2 tablespoons soft brown sugar
2 tablespoons single cream or evaporated milk
Pudding:
100 g (4 oz) self-raising flour
25 g (1 oz) cocoa
50 g (2 oz) butter or margarine
50 g (2 oz) caster sugar
1 egg
3 tablespoons milk
grated chocolate, to serve

Preparation time: 15 minutes
Cooking time: 1¼-1½ hours

1. Heat the butter, cocoa and brown sugar in a small saucepan and stir until smooth. Add the cream or evaporated milk, then pour into the base of a greased 600 ml (1 pint) pudding basin.

2. Sift the flour and cocoa into a mixing bowl. Add the butter and rub it into the flour until the mixture resembles fine breadcrumbs. Stir in the sugar.

3. Add the egg and milk, and mix to a soft, moist consistency. Add the mixture to the pudding basin and smooth the top.

4. Grease a piece of foil large enough to cover the basin and pleat the centre to allow for expansion. Cover the pudding with the foil, greased side down, and press closely against the sides of the basin.

5. Fill the base of a steamer with about 900 ml-1.2 litres (1½-2 pints) boiling water and steam the pudding for 1¼-1½ hours, until well risen and firm to the touch.

6. To unmould, place a serving dish over the pudding and turn both upside down. Shake the pudding free and lift off the basin. Serve hot with single cream or a pouring custard and sprinkle with grated chocolate.

 The fudge topping can be made in the morning. Cover with cling film.

Variation:
Chocolate chip pudding: Make the pudding in the same way as for Steamed fudge pudding. For the topping, omit the cocoa. For the pudding, replace the cocoa with an equal amount of self-raising flour and stir in 50 g (2 oz) cooking chocolate drops with the egg.

LEFT: Banana bavarois RIGHT: Steamed fudge pudding

CHOCOLATE CREAM PIE

100 g (4 oz) plain or white chocolate
50 ml (2 fl oz) water
2 teaspoons powdered gelatine
150 ml (¼ pint) single cream
icing sugar, to decorate
Pastry:
25 g (1 oz) caster sugar
40 g (1½ oz) butter
2 eggs, separated
65 g (2½ oz) plain flour

Preparation time: 15 minutes, plus resting and setting
Cooking time: 15-20 minutes
Oven: 200°C, 400°F, Gas Mark 6

1. To make the pastry, cream the sugar and butter until light and fluffy, then beat in 1 egg yolk. Gradually work in the flour to a soft, pliable dough. Knead lightly on a floured surface until smooth.
2. Roll the pastry out to fit a 15 cm (6 inch) fluted flan ring. Prick the base with a fork and rest for 30 minutes.
3. Grease a piece of foil to fit the flan ring and gently press the foil into the flan ring over the pastry. Bake blind in a preheated oven for 15-20 minutes until crisp and lightly coloured. Remove the foil for the last 5 minutes of cooking. Unmould and cool on a wire tray.
4. Reserve 1 square of chocolate and break the remainder into small pieces and place in a small heatproof bowl. Set the bowl over a saucepan of hot water until melted, stirring until smooth. Remove from the heat and beat in the remaining egg yolk.
5. Pour the water into a small heatproof bowl and sprinkle over the gelatine. Set the bowl over a pan of hot water and heat until dissolved. Stir into the chocolate mixture, then stir in the single cream. Cool until on the point of setting.
6. Whisk the egg whites until standing in soft peaks then gently fold into the chocolate mixture. Chill until set, about 2 hours.
7. Just before serving, pile the chocolate mixture into the pastry case and grate over the reserved chocolate. Decorate with icing sugar, if liked. Serve within 2 hours or the pastry will start to soften. F

F Thaw for 3 hours in the refrigerator.

APRICOT CHOCOLATE CHEESECAKE

Serves 6-8
1 × 200 g (7 oz) chocolate Swiss roll
2 × 420 g (14 oz) cans apricot halves
450 g (1 lb) curd cheese
3 tablespoons caster sugar
juice of half a lemon
2 eggs, separated
15 g (½ oz) powdered gelatine
150 ml (¼ pint) whipping cream
To decorate:
15 g (½ oz) plain cooking chocolate
10 g (¼ oz) butter or margarine

Preparation time: 25 minutes, plus setting

Be sure to do the feathered decoration immediately, before the cheesecake starts to set.

1. Cut the Swiss roll into 1 cm (½ inch) slices and use to line the sides and base of a 1.2 litre (2 pint) glass serving dish.
2. Drain the apricots and reserve 4 tablespoons of the juice. Reserve 4 apricot halves and purée the remainder.
3. In a large bowl, blend the curd cheese, sugar and lemon juice together, then gradually stir in the apricot purée. The resulting mixture should be smooth and runny. Beat in the egg yolks.
4. Place the reserved juice in a small heatproof bowl and sprinkle over the gelatine. Set the bowl over a pan of hot water and stir until dissolved. Blend into the cheesecake mixture and chill until on the point of setting, about 1 hour.
5. Whip the cream until it holds its shape on the whisk, then fold into the cheesecake mixture. Beat the egg whites until standing in soft peaks and carefully fold into the mixture. Pour the cheesecake filling over the Swiss roll and level with a spatula.
6. To decorate, melt the chocolate and butter in a small heatproof bowl set over a pan of hot water. Stir until smooth.
7. Fill a small greaseproof paper piping bag with the chocolate mixture and pipe parallel lines about 2.5 cm (1 inch) apart over the surface.
8. Turn the cheesecake 45° so the chocolate lines run horizontally, then draw the point of a sharp knife down across the lines about 2.5 cm (1 inch) apart.
9. Turn the cheesecake through 180° and draw the knife across the chocolate lines in the opposite direction to produce a feathered effect. F
10. Decorate with rosettes of cream if liked. Halve each reserved apricot, cut in a small fan shape and place on the cheesecake.

F Thaw for 6 hours in the refrigerator.

LEFT TO RIGHT: Chocolate cream pie; Apricot chocolate cheesecake; Hot chocolate trifle

HOT CHOCOLATE TRIFLE

1 × 200 g (7 oz) chocolate Swiss roll with vanilla filling
25 g (1 oz) plain chocolate, cut into small pieces
4 tablespoons medium sherry
300 ml (½ pint) milk
2 eggs
1 egg yolk
1 tablespoon caster sugar
few drops vanilla essence
To decorate:
25 g (1 oz) walnuts, chopped
25 g (1 oz) glacé cherries, chopped

Preparation time: 10 minutes
Cooking time: 1 hour
Oven: 180°C, 350°F, Gas Mark 4

1. Lightly grease a 600 ml (1 pint) transparent bowl or soufflé dish. Cut the Swiss roll into 1 cm (½ inch) slices and use to line the base and sides of the dish. Cut slices in half to fill any gaps.
2. Cube the remaining slices and layer with the chocolate in the bowl. Spoon the sherry over the Swiss roll.
3. To make the custard, warm the milk to blood heat. Beat the remaining ingredients together, then pour over the milk and mix well.
4. Strain the custard on to the Swiss roll and leave to stand for 30 minutes. Ⓐ
5. Place the trifle in a bain-marie, pour about 900 ml (1½ pints) water around the dish and bake in a pre-heated oven for 1 hour, or until the custard is set.
0. Sprinkle with the walnuts and cherries just before serving.

Ⓐ Make the pudding in the morning, cover and chill before baking.

DATE AND PECAN POTS

225 g (8 oz) medium fat soft cheese
50 g (2 oz) stoned dates, chopped
50 g (2 oz) pecan nut halves
100 g (4 oz) plain chocolate
1 lemon
1 tablespoon clear honey
15 g (½ oz) butter
2 teaspoons milk
icing sugar, for dusting

Preparation time: 15 minutes, plus setting

This dessert is best made a day in advance as the flavour improves on standing.

1. Cream the cheese until smooth, then add the dates.
2. Reserve 4 pecan halves for decoration and chop the remainder. Add to the cheese.
3. Grate 50 g (2 oz) of the chocolate and add to the cheese, together with the grated rind of the whole lemon, the juice of half the lemon and the honey. Stir until well mixed, then spoon into 4 individual ramekin dishes and smooth level.
4. Place the remaining chocolate, the butter and milk in a small heatproof bowl and set over a pan of hot water. Stir until smooth, then pour over to cover the surface of each ramekin dish. Place a pecan half in the centre of each and chill until set. Ⓕ
5. Before serving, line the ramekins in a row and place a piece of card with a straight side halving the ramekins over the top. Dust the uncovered halves with icing sugar then lift the card cleanly away.

Ⓐ To freeze, wrap the ramekins thoroughly in cling film to prevent dehydration. Thaw for 6 hours in the refrigerator before serving.

Strawberry cheesecake boxes

STRAWBERRY CHEESECAKE BOXES

Makes 9
butter, for greasing
1 egg
25 g (1 oz) caster sugar
25 g (1 oz) flour
1 tablespoon warm water
Filling:
150 ml (¼ pint) water
1 × 150 g (5 oz) packet strawberry jelly
juice of half a lemon
225 g (8 oz) full fat soft cheese
300 ml (½ pint) whipping cream
2 tablespoons redcurrant jelly, warmed
To decorate:
150 g (6 oz) plain chocolate or cooking chocolate,
  broken into pieces
9 candy strawberries or fresh strawberries

Preparation time: about 1 hour, plus setting
Cooking time: 10-12 minutes
Oven: 200°C, 400°F, Gas Mark 6

Vary the flavour of the cheesecake boxes by using a different flavoured jelly and appropriate decoration.

1. Line the base of an 18 cm (7 inch) square cake tin with lightly greased greaseproof paper.
2. Whisk the egg and sugar until light and foamy and the whisk leaves a trail when lifted.
3. Gently fold in the flour and water with a metal spoon, then pour into the prepared tin. Bake in a preheated oven for 10-12 minutes, until well risen and lightly golden brown. Turn out the cake and peel off the paper. Cool on a wire tray. Ⓐ
4. Heat the water, dissolve the jelly in it, then add the lemon juice. Chill until the mixture becomes syrupy, about 30 minutes.
5. Cream the cheese until smooth, then gradually add the jelly, beating well between each addition. Whip the cream, fold in two-thirds, then pour the mixture into an 18 cm (7 inch) square cake tin lined with greaseproof paper. Chill until set, about 2 hours. Ⓐ
6. Brush the sponge square with the redcurrant jelly then unmould the cheesecake on to the sponge. Peel off the paper and trim the edges if necessary. Ⓕ
7. Draw a 30 cm (12 inch) square on greaseproof paper. Melt the chocolate in a heatproof bowl set over a saucepan of hot water and stir until smooth. With a palette knife, spread the chocolate to fill the square. Cool until set. Ⓐ
8. Cut the chocolate into 36 equal squares then cut the cheesecake into nine 2-inch squares, trimming the edges if necessary. Working quickly to avoid over-handling the chocolate, press a piece of chocolate on to the 4 sides of each cheesecake square.
9. Pipe a generous ribbon of cream on top of each cheesecake using a star nozzle with a zig-zag motion. Decorate each with a strawberry.

Ⓐ The sponge base and filling can be made the day before. Make the chocolate squares 2-3 days in advance. Store in a rigid container in a cool place.
Ⓕ Thaw for four hours in the refrigerator.

QUICK CHOCOLATE MOUSSE

Serves 4-6
150 g (5 oz) plain chocolate, broken into pieces
1 teaspoon instant coffee powder or granules
1 tablespoon hot water
2 teaspoons Cointreau
4 eggs, separated
To decorate:
50 ml (2 fl oz) whipping cream
4 Chocolate leaves (page 7)

Preparation time: 15 minutes, plus chilling

1. Melt the chocolate in a heatproof mixing bowl set over a pan of hot water
2. Blend the instant coffee with the water, and add to the chocolate together with the Cointreau. Stir until smooth.
3. Remove from the pan and stir in the egg yolks.
4. Whisk the egg whites until stiff and fold carefully but thoroughly into the chocolate mixture.
5. Divide the mixture between individual ramekin dishes or glass bowls and chill for at least 2 hours or overnight. Ⓕ Do not use glass bowls if freezing.
6. Just before serving, pipe a rosette of cream on each mousse and decorate with a Chocolate leaf.

Ⓕ Can be kept frozen for up to 2 weeks. Thaw in the refrigerator for 4 hours and decorate just before serving.

ICED RUM AND RAISIN MOUSSE

75 g (3 oz) seedless raisins
4 tablespoons rum
100 g (4 oz) plain chocolate, broken into pieces
2 eggs, separated
150 ml (½ pint) double cream
To decorate:
65 ml (2½ fl oz) double cream, whipped
8 Chocolate cut-out shapes (page 8) (optional)

Preparation time: 10 minutes, plus soaking and freezing

1. Place the raisins in a small bowl and pour over the rum. Leave to stand for at least 8 hours or overnight.
2. Place the chocolate in a heatproof bowl and set over a saucepan of hot water. Stir until smooth.
3. Away from the heat, stir in the egg yolks, then add the raisins and rum.
4. Whip the cream until it just holds its shape on the whisk, then gently fold into the mixture.
5. Whisk the egg whites until standing in soft peaks then fold into the mixture.
6. Transfer the mixture to a 600 ml (1 pint) serving dish and place in the freezer for about 2 hours until just firm throughout. F
7. Stand in the refrigerator 15 minutes before serving.
8. Decorate with a shell border of cream and the chocolate shapes, if liked.

F Stand in the refrigerator for 2 hours before serving.

CHOCOLATE AND CINNAMON BREAD AND BUTTER PUDDING

4 slices of bread from a large loaf, crusts removed
25 g (1 oz) butter, softened
1 teaspoon ground cinnamon
40 g (1½ oz) sugar
3 eggs
600 ml (1 pint) milk
1 teaspoon instant coffee powder or granules
75 g (3 oz) plain chocolate, grated

Preparation time: 10 minutes, plus standing
Cooking time: 1¼-1½ hours
Oven: 180°C, 350°F, Gas Mark 4

1. Spread the sliced bread with the butter and sprinkle with the cinnamon. Cut each slice into 4 triangles.
2. Beat the sugar and eggs together in a mixing bowl. Heat the milk, coffee and half the chocolate to blood temperature. Whisk until well blended, then pour over the eggs. Mix well.
3. Layer the bread in a lightly greased 900 ml (1½ pint) pie dish and strain over the custard. Stand for 30 minutes. A
4. Place in a bain-marie, pour about 900 ml (1½ pints) water around the dish and bake in a preheated oven for 1¼-1½ hours or until the custard is set. 10 minutes before the end of the cooking time, sprinkle over the remaining chocolate.

A Make the pudding in the morning, cover and chill before baking.

SAXONY PUDDING

4 trifle sponges
8 small or 4 large almond macaroons
2-4 tablespoons medium sherry
2 eggs
1 egg yolk
1 tablespoon sugar
250 ml (8 fl oz) milk or milk and single cream mixed
100 g (4 oz) plain chocolate, broken into pieces
3 tablespoons single cream
25 g (1 oz) flaked almonds, toasted

Preparation time: 10 minutes, plus standing
Cooking time: about 1 hour
Oven: 180°C, 350°F, Gas Mark 4

1. Break up the sponges and macaroons and layer in a 600 ml (1 pint) soufflé dish. Spoon the sherry over the sponge and macaroons.
2. Beat the eggs, yolk and sugar together. Heat the milk to blood temperature, then mix well into the eggs.
3. Strain the custard into the soufflé dish and leave to stand for 30 minutes. A
4. Stand the pudding in a bain-marie, pour about 900 ml (1½ pints) water around the dish, and bake in a preheated oven for about 1 hour, or until firm.
5. Meanwhile, place the chocolate and cream in a small heatproof bowl and set over a pan of hot water. Stir vigorously until smooth, then keep warm.
6. Unmould the pudding, pour the chocolate sauce over the top and sprinkle with the almonds.

A Make the pudding in the morning, cover and chill before baking.

LEFT TO RIGHT: Iced rum and raisin mousse; Chocolate and cinnamon bread and butter pudding; Chocolate hearts

CHOCOLATE HEARTS

75 g (3 oz) plain chocolate, broken into pieces
225 g (8 oz) low fat soft cheese, sieved if necessary
1 tablespoon caster sugar
grated rind and juice of 1 orange
1 teaspoon powdered gelatine
65 ml (2½ fl oz) whipping cream
1 quantity Quick chocolate sauce (page 21) or
    150 ml (¼ pint) single cream, to serve
Chocolate cut-out shapes (page 8), to decorate

Preparation time: 15 minutes, plus cooling and setting

1. Place the chocolate in a heatproof bowl and set over a saucepan of hot water to melt. Stir until smooth.
2. Away from the heat, gradually spoon the cheese into the chocolate, beating well between each addition. Add the sugar and orange rind.
3. Place the orange juice in a small heatproof bowl and sprinkle over the gelatine. Set the bowl over the pan of hot water and stir until dissolved. Cool slightly, then add to the cheese mixture. Chill until on the point of setting, about 30 minutes.
4. Whip the cream and fold in to the mixture. Line 4 individual heart-shaped moulds with fine muslin and divide the mixture equally between them. Smooth and chill until set, about 2 hours. F
5. Carefully unmould the hearts on to a serving dish and peel off the muslin. Coat each heart with chocolate sauce or cream, and decorate with a chocolate shape. Serve with fresh orange segments.

F Thaw in the refrigerator for about 4 hours.

TRUFFLE JALOUSIE

225 g (8 oz) Madeira cake, crumbled
100 g (4 oz) almonds, chopped and toasted
5 tablespoons cocoa
50 g (2 oz) butter, softened
4 tablespoons mincemeat
1 egg
225 g (8 oz) puff pastry
milk or water, for brushing
butter, for greasing
icing sugar, for dusting

Preparation time: 15 minutes
Cooking time: 20-25 minutes
Oven: 220°C, 425°F, Gas Mark 7

1. Combine the cake crumbs, almonds, cocoa, butter, mincemeat and egg in a mixing bowl and beat until thoroughly blended.
2. Roll out the pastry on a lightly floured surface and trim to an oblong 28×33 cm (11×13 inches). With the blunt side of a knife, mark a line 7.5 cm (3 inches) in from each long edge.
3. With a sharp knife, cut 1 cm (½ inch) strips on the slant from the mark to the edge of the pastry.
4. Spread the filling down the centre of the pastry leaving a 1 cm (½ inch) gap between the filling and the cut in the pastry. Lightly brush the pastry surrounding the filling with milk or water.
5. To seal the ends, fold the two short ends about 2.5 cm (1 inch) over the filling. Place the pastry strips alternately from each side over the filling to form a plait. Press down lightly.
6. With a large slice or spatula, carefully lift the plait on to a greased baking sheet and bake in a preheated oven for 20 minutes until the pastry is well risen and lightly golden brown.
7. Sprinkle the plait generously with icing sugar and return to the oven for a further 5 minutes until the sugar has melted to a shiny glaze.
8. Remove immediately on to a cooling rack and cool. ⅀ Serve cold cut into fingers.

⅀ Reheat from frozen in a preheated oven before serving.

PROFITEROLES WITH CHOCOLATE SAUCE

Choux pastry:
150 ml (¼ pint) water
50 g (2 oz) butter
65 g (2½ oz) flour, sieved
2 eggs
Filling:
2 tablespoons instant custard powder
1 tablespoon cocoa
1 tablespoon sugar
300 ml (½ pint) milk
150 ml (¼ pint) double cream, whipped
1 quantity Special chocolate sauce (page 21)

Preparation time: 20 minutes, plus cooling
Cooking time: 25-30 minutes
Oven: 200°C, 400°F, Gas Mark 6

1. Heat the water and butter in a small pan. When melted, bring to the boil. Remove from the heat and add the flour all at once. Beat vigorously with a wooden spoon until the paste leaves the sides of the pan and forms a smooth ball. Cool slightly.
2. Beat in the eggs, one at a time, until the mixture becomes smooth and glossy.
3. Sprinkle 2 large baking sheets with a little cold water; this assists the choux balls to rise and become puffed.
4. Fill a large nylon piping bag fitted with a large plain nozzle with the choux pastry, and pipe about 24 equal-sized bulbs on to the baking sheets. Bake in a preheated oven for about 30 minutes, until well risen and golden brown.
5. Quickly split each choux ball with a knife and return to the oven to dry out. ⅀
6. Blend the custard powder, cocoa and sugar with a little of the milk. Bring the remaining milk to the boil. Pour over the custard, stir well and return to the rinsed pan. Return to the boil, stirring constantly and cook for 2-3 minutes. Tip into a clean bowl to cool. Cover closely with cling film to prevent a skin forming.
7. Blend the custard and cream together in a liquidizer to smooth out any lumps. Fill a large piping bag, fitted with a large plain nozzle, with the mixture and fill each choux bun.
8. Place the filled buns on a large glass serving dish. Pour over a little of the chocolate sauce and serve the rest separately.

⅀ The unfilled choux balls can be frozen, well wrapped, until required.

LEFT: Profiteroles with chocolate sauce RIGHT: Truffle jalousie

GÂTEAUX

WINDMILL CAKE

Makes one 20 cm (8 inch) cake
½ quantity Chocolate victoria sandwich mixture (page 51)
½ quantity Chocolate victoria sandwich mixture (page 51),
    replacing the cocoa with flour
about 6 tablespoons seedless raspberry jelly, melted
255 g (8 oz) butter or block margarine
450 g (1 lb) icing sugar, sifted
2 tablespoons peppermint essence
2 tablespoons cocoa
2 tablespoons boiling water
24 chocolate buttons or Chocolate cut-out shapes
    (page 8), to decorate (optional)

Preparation time: about 25 minutes
Cooking time: 25-30 minutes
Oven: 180°C, 350°F, Gas Mark 4

This cake is best assembled when the Victoria sandwich layers have been made 2-3 days in advance and stored in an airtight container.

1. Prepare and cook the 2 Victoria sandwich layers in 20 cm (8 inch) round sandwich tins as directed on page 51.
2. Cut out 2 circular cardboard discs, 5 cm (2 inches) and 14 cm (5½ inches) in diameter, as templates.
3. Place the small template on one cake layer and cut round it. Place the large template on the same cake and cut round that. Carefully free the circles of cake. Repeat this process with the other cake layer.
4. Reassemble the cake layers alternating the plain and chocolate circles. Brush each ring edge with a little warmed jelly to stick them together.
5. Cream the butter or margarine and half the icing sugar until light and fluffy. Beat in the remaining sugar. Divide the mixture into two-third and one-third portions in separate bowls.
6. Flavour the small portion by beating in the peppermint essence. Blend the cocoa with the water and cool. Beat the cocoa into the large portion of butter cream.
7. Sandwich the cake layers together with one-third of the chocolate butter cream.
8. Divide the cake top and sides into 8 sections and pipe stars with the 2 kinds of butter cream to fill each section in alternating flavours. Finish the cake edges with the chocolate buttons or Chocolate cut-out shapes, if liked.

CHOCOLATE MERINGUE LAYER

Serves 6-8
120 g (4½ oz) icing sugar
2 egg whites
1 teaspoon vanilla essence
Filling:
100 g (4 oz) almonds, finely chopped and toasted
½ quantity hot Crème ganache (page 38)
1 teaspoon instant coffee powder or granules
1 tablespoon boiling water
2 tablespoons Cointreau, rum or brandy
150 ml (¼ pint) double or whipping cream
To decorate:
50 ml (2 fl oz) double or whipping cream
Chocolate curls (page 7)

Preparation time: 30 minutes, plus cooling
Cooking time: 1½-2 hours
Oven: 150°C, 300°F, Gas Mark 2

1. Draw an 18 cm (7 inch) diameter circle on 3 separate sheets of non-stick silicone paper. Place on 2 baking sheets.
2. Put the icing sugar, egg whites and vanilla essence into a large bowl set over a saucepan of hot water. Whisk until the mixture becomes thick and glossy, and stands in stiff peaks. Remove from the heat and beat until cool.
3. Divide the mixture into 3 portions, spoon into the circles drawn on the paper and spread evenly with a spatula. Bake in two batches in a preheated oven for about 1½-2 hours, until crisp and thoroughly dried out. Carefully remove the non-stick silicone paper and cool the meringue on a wire tray. Ⓐ
4. To make the filling, beat the almonds into the Crème ganache. Blend the coffee with the boiling water and beat into the chocolate mixture with the alcohol. Chill for 4 hours.
5. Beat the filling well, whip the cream, then fold the cream into the filling. Divide into 2 portions and use to sandwich the meringue layers together.
6. To decorate, whip the cream then spread on top of the gâteau and decorate with the chocolate scrolls.

Ⓐ Meringue cases keep up to 3 weeks in an airtight tin. When filled, eat on the same day.

LEFT: Windmill cake RIGHT: Chocolate meringue layer

CRÈME GANACHE

300 g (11 oz) plain chocolate, broken into pieces
150 ml (¼ pint) double or whipping cream

Preparation time: 10 minutes

1. Place the chocolate in a heatproof bowl and set over a pan of hot water. When melted, stir until smooth.
2. Meanwhile, pour the cream into a separate pan and bring to the boil.
3. Gradually pour the cream into the melted chocolate, stirring vigorously until smooth.

To use Crème ganache:
1. Use immediately, while still hot, to pour over a sponge to give a coating that will set.
2. Cool for 1-2 hours until thickened, then beat and combine with whipped cream to use as a filling and coating.
3. Cool, then chill about 4 hours until set to a firm paste which can be beaten and used as a filling or piped for decoration.

LEFT: Tipsy cake RIGHT: Ganache torte

TIPSY CAKE

Serves 6-8
150 g (5 oz) self-raising flour
25 g (1 oz) cocoa
175 g (6 oz) soft margarine, plus extra for greasing
175 g (6 oz) caster sugar
3 eggs
1×411 g (14 oz) can red or black pitted cherries
8 tablespoons medium sherry
450 ml (¾ pint) double or whipping cream
Chocolate leaves, to decorate (page 7)

Preparation time: 25 minutes, plus cooling
Cooking time: 35-40 minutes
Oven: 180°C, 350°F, Gas Mark 4

1. Sift the flour and cocoa into a mixing bowl and add the margarine, sugar and eggs. Beat well with a wooden spoon until thoroughly blended, then spoon into a greased 1.2 litre (2 pint) ring mould. Smooth the mixture level with a spatula.
2. Bake in a preheated oven for 35-40 minutes until the cake is well risen and springs back when pressed with a finger. Turn out and cool on a wire tray. F
3. With a sharp knife, cut a slice 2.5 cm (1 inch) deep off the top of the ring. Lift off the slice carefully and reserve.
4. With a teaspoon, scoop out some of the cake in the bottom layer to form a hollow 1 cm (½ inch) deep and 2.5 cm (1 inch) wide. Transfer the bottom layer to a serving dish.
5. Drain the cherries and reserve 4 tablespoons of the juice. Mix the juice with 6 tablespoons of the sherry and spoon over the bottom layer.
6. Whip the cream with the remaining sherry until stiff. Spread a quarter of the cream in the hollow. Reserve 8 cherries for decoration and spoon the others evenly over the cream.
7. Place the top of the cake ring over the cherries and smooth the remaining cream all over the ring to cover it entirely. A Decorate with the reserved cherries and chocolate leaves.

F Thaw for 4 hours at room temperature and continue from step 3.
A Can be made the day before.

GANACHE TORTE

Makes one 20 cm (8 inch) torte
4 eggs, separated
100 g (4 oz) caster sugar, plus 1 tablespoon
50 g (2 oz) plain flour
50 g (2 oz) cornflour
50 g (2 oz) granulated sugar
50 ml (2 fl oz) water
3 tablespoons rum
150 ml (¼ pint) double or whipping cream
1 quantity Crème ganache (page 38), cool but still soft butter, for greasing
To decorate:
12 small Chocolate wedges (page 7)
Chocolate scrolls (page 8)

Preparation time: 30 minutes
Cooking time: about 20 minutes
Oven: 180°C, 350°F, Gas Mark 4

1. Place the egg yolks and 100 g (4 oz) of the sugar in a large mixing bowl set over a pan of hot, not boiling, water. Whisk until the mixture becomes light, foamy and creamy.
2. Sift the flours together. Whisk the egg whites and the remaining tablespoon caster sugar until standing in soft peaks, then fold into the egg yolk mixture with the flour. Using a large metal spoon, make a figure-of-eight cutting action to fold the mixture lightly but thoroughly until evenly blended.
3. Divide the mixture between two 20 cm (8 inch) deep greased sandwich tins. Smooth level with a spatula, then bake in a preheated oven for about 20 minutes, until well risen and golden brown. Turn out and cool on a wire tray. F Slice each sandwich into 2 layers.
4. Dissolve the granulated sugar in the water over a gentle heat, then bring to the boil. Away from the heat, stir in the rum, then spoon over the cake layers.
5. Whip the cream and beat half into the Crème ganache. Use one-third to sandwich the layers of cake together, ending with a layer of cake. Press down well.
6. Use the remaining Crème ganache to cover the entire gâteau, smoothing it evenly. If liked, use a serrated comb or knife to ridge the sides of the cake. When set, mark the top of the gâteau into 12 sections with a sharp knife. Pipe a small rosette of the remaining cream in each section and one in the centre.
7. Press a chocolate wedge into each rosette and sprinkle chocolate scrolls over the centre rosette. This torte is best eaten the same day.

F Thaw for 1 hour at room temperature, then continue the recipe from step 3, above.

MOCHA CHEESECAKE

Makes one 23 cm (9 inch) cake
175 g (6 oz) digestive biscuits, crushed
50 g (2 oz) butter, melted
100 g (4 oz) butter
75 g (3 oz) caster sugar
2 eggs, separated
5 teaspoons instant coffee powder or granules
2 tablespoons boiling water
½ teaspoon vanilla essence
4 tablespoons single cream or top of the milk
1 tablespoon cornflour
450 g (1 lb) curd cheese
100 g (4 oz) plain or bitter chocolate, coarsely chopped
To decorate:
a little icing sugar
25 g (1 oz) plain chocolate, finely grated

Preparation time: 25-30 minutes
Cooking time: 1 hour
Oven: 160°C, 325°F, Gas Mark 3

1. Stir the biscuit crumbs into the melted butter and mix thoroughly. Press the mixture into the base of a 23 cm (9 inch) springform or loose-bottomed cake tin.
2. Cream the butter and sugar until light and fluffy, then beat in the egg yolks one at a time.
3. Blend the coffee with the water and add to the mixture with the vanilla essence, cream or top of the milk and cornflour. Mix well.
4. Beat the curd cheese into the mixture together with the chocolate and mix well.
5. Whisk the egg whites until standing in soft peaks and carefully fold into the mixture.
6. Pour the mixture over the biscuit base and smooth level with a spatula. Bake in a preheated oven for 1 hour, or until set. Turn off the oven and leave the cheesecake in the oven to cool. (It will rise slightly during cooking, but will fall on cooling.)
7. To decorate, place a 10 cm (4 inch) diameter disc of paper or card in the centre of the cheesecake and dust the cake with icing sugar. Carefully remove the disc and spoon the grated chocolate into the centre.

> To obtain neat orange slices without any pith on them, cut a slice off the top and bottom of each orange and stand it on a board. With a small serrated knife, make smooth downward cuts following the curve of the orange. When you have been round the orange once, repeat the process to make sure all the pith has been removed.

LEFT: Mocha cheesecake RIGHT: Chocolate savarin

CHOCOLATE SAVARIN

butter, for greasing
120 g (4½ oz) strong plain flour
20 g (¾ oz) fresh yeast or 2 teaspoons dried yeast
15 g (½ oz) caster sugar
4 tablespoons milk, warmed to blood heat
2 eggs, beaten
45 g (1¾ oz) butter
Syrup:
100 g (4 oz) sugar
150 ml (¼ pint) water
1 tablespoon instant coffee powder or granules
1 tablespoon cocoa
2 tablespoons hot water
2 tablespoons brandy or cognac
4 oranges, peeled, pith removed and sliced
julienne strips of orange, to decorate

Preparation time: 15 minutes, plus approximately
1-1½ hours rising
Cooking time: 30-40 minutes
Oven: 200°C, 400°F, Gas Mark 6

1. Grease a 1.2 litre (2 pint) savarin or ring mould with butter.
2. Sift the flour into a warm bowl.
3. Cream the fresh yeast with 1 teaspoon of the sugar and gradually add the warm milk, then the eggs. If using dried yeast, sprinkle the yeast over the warmed milk and add one teaspoon of the sugar. Stand in a warm place covered with a cloth for 15 minutes until frothy, then beat in the eggs.
4. Tip the liquid into the flour and beat with a wooden spoon for 5 minutes, or 1 minute in an electric mixer. Cover the bowl with a damp cloth and stand it in a warm place until the mixture doubles in bulk, about 40 minutes.
5. Cream the butter with the remaining sugar until soft and light, then beat into the mixture for 5 minutes, or 1 minute in an electric mixer.
6. Pour the batter into the tin and stand in a warm place until the mixture has risen to the top of the tin. Bake in a preheated oven for about 20-30 minutes, until the savarin is browned and springs back when lightly pressed with a finger.
7. Meanwhile, to make the syrup, beat the sugar and water in a heavy-based pan until dissolved. Simmer for 5 minutes.
8. Blend the coffee and cocoa with the water and stir into the syrup. Add the brandy or cognac.
9. Loosen the savarin from the tin. While it is still warm, make a few holes in it with a fine skewer and spoon over the syrup until thoroughly soaked.
10. Carefully turn out on to a serving dish and cool. Arrange the orange slices in the centre of the savarin and decorate with the julienne strips.

CHOCOLATE SLICE

Serves 8

butter, for greasing
3 eggs
75 g (3 oz) caster sugar
75 g (3 oz) plain flour
1 tablespoon warm water
2 quantities Special butter cream (page 43) flavoured with 6 tablespoons cocoa
75 g (3 oz) almonds, chopped and toasted

Preparation time: 30 minutes, plus cooling
Cooking time: 10-12 minutes
Oven: 200°C, 400°F, Gas Mark 6

1. Line a 23×33 cm (9×13 inch) Swiss roll tin with greased greaseproof paper.
2. Using an electric beater, whisk the eggs and caster sugar until thick and foamy, and the whisk leaves a trail in the mixture when lifted.
3. Carefully fold in the sifted flour and the water.

4. Pour the mixture into the prepared tin and smooth evenly with a spatula. Bake in a preheated oven for 10-12 minutes, or until well risen and golden brown. Turn out on to a wire tray, peel off the lining paper and leave to cool.
5. Cut into 3 equal sections, cutting across width of the cake. Ⓐ
6. Sandwich the cake sections together with one-third of the butter cream. Press down well.
7. Spread the sides with half the remaining butter cream and coat with the chopped almonds.
8. Spread a little more of the butter cream on top and smooth. With a small plain nozzle, pipe the remaining butter cream in diagonal parallel lines across the top of the slice. Finish with a shell border using a small star nozzle.

This slice is best eaten on the day it is made.

Ⓐ Can be made in the morning and covered with cling film.

TOP: Chocolate slice BOTTOM: Praline roll

PRALINE ROLL

Serves 6-8
butter, for greasing
3 eggs
75 g (3 oz) caster sugar
75 g (3 oz) plain flour
1 tablespoon warm water
caster sugar, for sprinkling
Filling:
½ quantity Praline (page 49), crushed
1 quantity Special butter cream
Icing:
175 g (6 oz) icing sugar, sifted
3 tablespoons cocoa
1½ tablespoons water or rum

Preparation time: 30 minutes, plus cooling and chilling
Cooking time: 20 minutes
Oven: 200°C, 400°F, Gas Mark 6

1. Grease and line a 28×33 cm (11×13 inch) Swiss roll tin with greaseproof paper.
2. Make a 3-egg fatless sponge mixture, as in steps 2 and 3 of the Chocolate slice recipe (page 42).
3. Pour the mixture into the prepared Swiss roll tin and tilt the tin until the mixture is evenly spread. Bake in a preheated oven for 10-12 minutes, until the sponge is well risen and golden brown, and springs back when lightly pressed with a finger.
4. Turn the Swiss roll out on a sheet of greaseproof paper dusted with caster sugar and peel off the lining paper.
5. Trim the crusty edges then, with the blunt edge of a knife, mark a line approximately 2.5 cm (1 inch) in from one of the short edges. Roll up the Swiss roll with the greaseproof paper from the marked edge. Leave to cool.
6. When cold, carefully unroll the sponge and remove the greaseproof paper.
7. Beat the Praline into two-thirds of the butter cream. Spread this filling evenly over the sponge to within 1 cm (½ inch) of each edge. Roll the sponge up tightly and chill for about 1 hour. F
8. Mix together the icing sugar and cocoa and stir in the water or rum to make a thick icing which coats the back of a spoon. Stand the sponge on a wire tray and pour over the icing, spreading it evenly with a spatula.
9. Immediately transfer the cake to a serving dish and leave to set. When set, pipe scrolls across the top with the remaining butter cream, using a star nozzle. A

F Thaw for about 4 hours in the refrigerator.
A Can be made in the morning.

SPECIAL BUTTER CREAM

50 g (2 oz) sugar
150 ml (¼ pint) water
1 egg yolk
150 g (5 oz) unsalted butter, cut into small pieces

Preparation time: 15 minutes, plus cooling
Cooking time: about 8 minutes

1. Place the sugar and water in a small saucepan and heat gently until the sugar is dissolved.
2. Increase the heat, and boil rapidly for about 3 minutes without stirring. Continue boiling to 107°C, 225°F or until the thread stage is achieved – the syrup forms a thread when allowed to drop from a spoon on to a plate.
3. Place the egg yolk in a mixing bowl, gradually pour on the syrup and beat until the mixture cools.
4. Gradually beat in the butter, a little at a time, until smooth. Chill if necessary to firm the mixture.

WHISKED FATLESS SPONGE

Makes two 20 cm (8 inch) sandwich cakes
lard, butter or margarine, melted, for brushing
flour, for dusting
4 eggs
100 g (4 oz) caster sugar
100 g (4 oz) plain flour

Preparation time: about 15 minutes
Cooking time: 15-20 minutes
Oven: 180°C, 350°F, Gas Mark 4

1. Brush two 20 cm (8 inch) deep-sided sandwich tins with melted fat and dust with flour.
2. Using an electric beater, whisk the eggs and sugar until the mixture becomes very thick and light, and leaves a trail when the whisk is lifted.
3. Sift the flour over the surface of the mixture. With a metal spoon, fold in the flour using a cutting figure-of-eight action until all the flour has been incorporated; fold as lightly and as little as possible.
4. Pour the mixture into the prepared tins and tilt until the mixture spreads evenly over the tins.
5. Bake in a preheated oven for 15-20 minutes until the sponge is well risen and golden brown, and springs back when lightly pressed with a finger. Turn out and cool on a wire tray.

ORANGE TRUFFLE CAKE

Makes one 20 cm (8 inch) cake
grated rind of 1 orange
1 quantity Genoese sponge mixture (page 45)
butter, for greasing
Filling:
150 ml (¼ pint) double or whipping cream
150 g (5 oz) plain chocolate, broken into pieces
1 tablespoon Cointreau (optional)
Frosting:
50 g (2 oz) butter
50 g (2 oz) soft brown sugar
grated rind of 1 orange
2 tablespoons orange juice
225 g (8 oz) icing sugar, sifted
To decorate:
Chocolate scrolls (page 8)
icing sugar

Preparation time: about 25 minutes, plus cooling
Cooking time: 20 minutes
Oven: 180°C, 350°C, Gas Mark 4

1. Fold the orange rind into the sponge mixture with the flour. Bake the orange genoese sponge in two 20 cm (8 inch) greased sandwich tins in a preheated oven for about 20 minutes, until the sponge is well risen, golden brown and springs back when lightly pressed with a finger. Turn out and cool on a wire tray. Ⓐ
2. Meanwhile, bring the cream just to the boil. Away from the heat, stir in the chocolate and continue stirring as the chocolate melts until the mixture is smooth and thick. Stir in the Cointreau, if using. Cool and chill until set, about 4 hours. Ⓐ
3. When the truffle filling has set, spread over one sponge layer and place the second layer on top. Press down lightly.
4. In a separate pan, combine the butter, soft brown sugar, orange rind and juice. Heat gently until the butter has melted and the sugar is dissolved, then boil for 1 minute. Ⓐ
5. Pour the mixture into the icing sugar and stir with a wooden spoon, gradually incorporating all the icing sugar. Beat well until smooth, then spoon over the cake and smooth with a palette knife. Decorate with Chocolate scrolls and dust lightly with icing sugar.

Ⓐ The sponge can be made in the morning, and covered with cling film.
Ⓐ The filling can be made in the morning. Cover with cling film and chill.

VALENTINE GÂTEAU

Makes one 18 cm (7 inch) gâteau
butter, for greasing
25 g (1 oz) hazelnuts, finely ground
1 quantity Genoese sponge mixture (page 45)
300 ml (½ pint) whipping cream
50 g (2 oz) plain chocolate, grated
225 g (8 oz) firm strawberries
½ quantity hot Crème ganache (page 38)
Chocolate leaves, to decorate (page 7)
icing sugar, for dusting (optional)

Preparation time: 50 minutes, plus cooling
Cooking time: 15-20 minutes
Oven: 180°C, 350°F, Gas Mark 4

1. Grease and flour two 18 cm (7 inch) heart-shaped tins, measured at the widest part.
2. Fold the hazelnuts into the sponge mixture with the flour. Bake in a preheated oven for 15-20 minutes until well risen and golden brown and the sponge springs back when lightly pressed with a finger. Turn out on to a wire tray and cool. Ⓕ
3. When cool, split each heart into 2 layers. Whip the cream, fold in the grated chocolate and spread one-third of the cream on one heart.
4. Reserve 3 strawberries with stalks on for decoration, then slice some of the remaining even-sized strawberries to obtain 24 thin slices. Roughly chop the remainder.
5. Spread the chopped strawberries over the first layer of cream then smooth over a little more cream and sandwich with a second layer of sponge. Portion the remaining cream in two and sandwich the remaining sponges with the cream ending with a layer of sponge.
6. Stand the gâteau on a wire tray and pour over the Crème ganache. Smooth over quickly with a small palette knife. Leave to set for about 15 minutes.
7. Arrange the sliced strawberries in a row around the base of the gâteau. Place the 3 whole strawberries in a cluster on top of the gâteau and surround with Chocolate leaves.
8. Leave the gâteau to set for about 2 hours. Ⓐ If liked, give it a very light sprinkling of icing sugar just before serving. Once assembled, this gâteau is best eaten on the day it is made.

Ⓕ Thaw for 1 hour at room temperature.
Ⓐ Can be made in the morning.

LEFT: Orange truffle cake   RIGHT: Valentine gâteau

GENOESE SPONGE

Makes two 20 cm (8 inch) sandwich cakes

lard, butter or margarine, melted, for brushing
flour, for dusting
4 eggs
100 g (4 oz) caster sugar
100 g (4 oz) plain flour
25 g (1 oz) butter, melted

Preparation time: about 15 minutes
Cooking time: 15-20 minutes
Oven: 180°C, 350°F, Gas Mark 4

1. Brush two 20 cm (8 inch) deep-sided sandwich tins with melted fat and dust with flour.
2. Using an electric beater, whisk the eggs and sugar until the mixture becomes very thick and light, and leaves a trail when the whisk is lifted.
3. Sift half the flour over the surface of the mixture. Add half the melted butter. With a metal spoon, fold in the flour using a cutting figure-of-eight action until all the flour has been incorporated. Repeat with the remaining flour and butter. Fold as lightly and as little as possible.
4. Pour the mixture into the prepared tins and tilt until the mixture spreads evenly over the tins.
5. Bake in a preheated oven for 15-20 minutes until the sponge is well risen and golden brown, and springs back when lightly pressed with a finger. Turn out and cool on a wire tray.

MERINGUE BASKET

Serves 8-10
4 egg whites
100 g (4 oz) caster sugar
100 g (4 oz) icing sugar
2 tablespoons cocoa, sieved
1 teaspoon vanilla essence
Filling:
200 g (7 oz) plain chocolate, broken into pieces
1 tablespoon milk
4 egg yolks
2 tablespoons liqueur, e.g. Cointreau, Tia Maria
450 ml (¾ pint) double or whipping cream
25 g (1 oz) chocolate vermicelli (optional)
225 g (8 oz) fresh raspberries
25 g (1 oz) cooking chocolate, to decorate

Preparation time: about 35 minutes, plus cooling
Cooking time: 3 hours
Oven: 110°C, 225°F, Gas Mark ¼

Vary the fruit with soft fruit in season. Do not use tinned or frozen fruit as the juices will make the mixture soggy.

1. Draw four 18 cm (7 inch) squares on 4 separate pieces of non-stick silicone paper. Lay a piece of paper on each of 2 baking sheets.
2. Beat the egg whites until standing in stiff peaks. Add all the caster sugar and continue beating until very stiff and standing in rigid peaks.
3. Carefully fold in the icing sugar, cocoa and vanilla.
4. Spoon the meringue into a piping bag fitted with a 1 cm (½ inch) plain nozzle. Pipe straight lines to form a square on the non-stick silicone paper on the baking sheets, using the drawing as a guide. Spoon more meringue in the centre of each square and spread it with a spatula to form 2 solid squares of meringue. Spread the meringue up to the level of the piping.
5. Bake in a preheated oven for 1½-2 hours until completely dried out. Peel off the paper and cool.
6. Pipe the outline only of the squares on the 2 remaining sheets of paper. Bake and cool as before. Use up any remaining meringue mixture by piping ribbons of meringue around and inside the square outline to use as decoration. A
7. To make the filling, melt the chocolate and milk in a heatproof bowl set over a pan of hot water. Stir until smooth. Away from the heat, add the egg yolks one at a time, stirring well after each addition. Stir in the liqueur. Cool until set, about 2 hours.
8. About 1 hour before serving, whip the cream and spread 2 tablespoons of cream over a solid base meringue and fit a square outline over the top. Spread a little more cream over the square outline and top with the remaining square outline.

9. Mask the sides of the meringue basket with cream and draw a serrated scraper across each side to form a ridged surface.
10. With a small palette knife, press on a narrow band of chocolate vermicelli about 1 cm (½ inch) from the bottom of the basket.
11. Carefully transfer to a serving plate. Spoon the filling into the base. Reserve 12 raspberries for decoration and arrange the remainder on top of the filling.
12. Mask one side of the remaining solid square of meringue with a thin layer of cream and position over the basket, cream side up. Spoon the remaining cream into a large piping bag fitted with a 3 mm (⅛ inch) plain nozzle. Pipe a series of parallel lines in one direction over the top of the basket.
13. Melt the cooking chocolate in a heatproof bowl set over a pan of hot water. Spoon the chocolate into a small greaseproof paper bag and snip the end to make a very small aperture. Drizzle the chocolate over the surface of the basket.
14. Decorate with the reserved raspberries and meringue ribbons.

Variation:
PETITS VACHERINS
Using a ½ quantity of the meringue mixture above, spoon the mixture into a piping bag fitted with a 1 cm (½ inch) star nozzle. Pipe small nests no more than 4 cm (1½ inches) in diameter on to baking sheets lined with non-stick silicone paper. Bake as above.

Using 200 ml (8 fl oz) double or whipping cream, whipped, pipe a swirl of cream into each vacherin. Top each with a small strawberry, quartered, mandarin orange segments, or grated chocolate.

A Meringue cases keep up to 3 weeks in an airtight tin. When filled, eat on same day.

1. Fitting the square outline meringue shapes.

2. Making a ridged surface around the basket.

3. Spooning filling into the assembled basket

CROWNING GLORY

Serves 8-10
225 g (8 oz) plain chocolate, broken into pieces
50 g (2 oz) butter, plus extra for greasing
2 eggs
175 g (6 oz) bourbon biscuits, crushed
50 g (2 oz) hazelnuts, chopped and toasted
50 g (2 oz) glacé cherries, quartered
2 tablespoons rum
To decorate:
150 ml (¼ pint) double or whipping cream, whipped
6 glacé cherries

Preparation time: 20 minutes, plus chilling

1. Melt the chocolate and butter together in a heat-proof bowl set over hot water. Stir vigorously until smooth.
2. Beat the eggs in a large bowl, then gradually add the chocolate mixture a little at a time and stir vigorously until blended.
3. Stir the biscuits, nuts, glacé cherries and rum into the chocolate mixture, then spoon into a buttered 600 ml (1 pint) ring mould. Chill until set, about 4 hours.
4. Unmould the cake by dipping the base of the mould in hot water for 10 seconds. Avoid letting any water run over the mixture. Invert a serving dish over the gâteau then turn both upside down. Lift off the mould. F
5. To decorate, pipe 6 large rosettes of cream on top of the gâteau and top each with a cherry.

F Thaw for 4 hours in the refrigerator.

PARIS BREST AU CHOCOLAT

Serves 4-6
1 quantity Choux pastry (page 35)
25 g (1 oz) flaked almonds
icing sugar, for dusting
Filling:
150 ml (¼ pint) milk
1 tablespoon instant custard powder
75 g (3 oz) plain chocolate, broken into pieces
250 ml (8 fl oz) double cream, whipped
½ quantity Praline (page 49) (optional)

Preparation time: 20 minutes
Cooking time: about 40 minutes
Oven: 200°C, 400°F, Gas Mark 6;
 then 190°C, 375°F, Gas Mark 5

Choux pastry, once filled, is best eaten on the day it is made, otherwise the pastry will become soggy.

1. Spoon the Choux pastry into a large piping bag fitted with a 2 cm (¾ inch) nozzle.
2. On a greased baking sheet pipe a thick fat circle of pastry about 20 cm (8 inch) in diameter.
3. Sprinkle the pastry with the flaked almonds, then dust with icing sugar. Bake in a preheated oven for 15 minutes, then reduce the heat and bake for a further 15-20 minutes until the ring is well risen. Cover the ring loosely with foil if the almonds brown too quickly during the cooking time.
4. When cooked, split the ring open and return to the oven for 5 minutes to dry out.
5. To make the filling, blend the milk and custard powder, pour into a pan and bring to the boil, stirring constantly. Cool slightly, then cover closely with cling film to prevent a skin forming. Leave until cold.
6. Place the chocolate in a small heatproof bowl and set over a pan of hot water to melt.
7. Stir the melted chocolate into the custard. When smooth, fold in the cream and lastly the Praline, if using. Place the base of the choux ring on a serving dish and spoon on the chocolate filling. Replace the top and dust with icing sugar.

Variation:
Pipe small rings of Choux pastry about 10 cm (4 inches) in diameter. Prepare, bake and fill in the same way as above.

TOP: Paris brest au chocolat BOTTOM: Crowning glory

PRALINE

Makes about 225 g (8 oz)
butter, for greasing
100 g (4 oz) caster sugar
100 g (4 oz) unskinned almonds

Preparation time: 5 minutes
Cooking time: about 10-15 minutes

Praline is normally made with almonds, but is also delicious made with hazelnuts, walnuts, pecans or pistachio nuts. Care should be taken not to burn the nuts when placed in the caramelized sugar. Keep a wooden spatula or spoon and a plate on which to put the spoon handy to turn the nuts frequently.

1. Grease a heatproof plate, tin or marble slab with butter.
2. Sprinkle the sugar evenly over the base of a heavy saucepan or frying pan. Stand the pan over a gentle heat and heat the sugar until it caramelizes. Avoid stirring the sugar at this stage, though this may be necessary if it becomes overheated.
3. When the sugar has melted and is golden, stir in the nuts. Still over a low heat, turn the nuts until they are toasted on both sides, then pour on to the heatproof plate. When the praline is completely cold, break it into pieces.

TOP: Chocolate basket BOTTOM: Chocolate bran cake

CHOCOLATE BASKET

Makes one 20 cm (8 inch) gâteau

1 quantity Chocolate victoria sandwich mixture (page 51), baked in two 20 cm (8 inch) sandwich tins
2 quantities Chocolate butter cream (page 51)
about 24 Chocolate leaves (page 7)
about 12 glacé cherries, some halved and some quartered
icing sugar, for dusting (optional)

Preparation time: 1 hour
Cooking time: 25-30 minutes

1. Cut each cake into 2 layers. Sandwich 3 layers together, using 3 tablespoons of butter cream for each layer, ending with a layer of butter cream.

2. Using a small teaplate as a guide, cut a disc about 15 cm (6 inches) in diameter out of the top cake layer. Coat the top with a thin layer of butter cream and place the outer ring on the top of the cake.

3. Fill a cake decorating bag with the remaining icing and fit with a ribbon nozzle. Pipe a basketwork design on the sides of the cake and on the top and side of the 15 cm (6 inch) layer of cake.

4. Carefully arrange the chocolate leaves over the rim all round the cake. Position the glacé cherries at intervals.

5. Carefully lower the small layer on top of the cake and lightly dust with icing sugar, if liked.

CHOCOLATE BRAN CAKE

25 g (1 oz) bran
100 g (4 oz) sultanas
100 ml (3½ fl oz) orange juice
200 g (7 oz) self-raising flour
25 g (1 oz) cocoa
75 g (3 oz) block margarine, plus extra for greasing
50 g (2 oz) soft brown sugar
50 g (2 oz) walnuts, chopped
½ teaspoon ground nutmeg
2 eggs
Filling and Topping: (optional)
100 g (4 oz) curd cheese
75 g (3 oz) plain chocolate
walnut halves
icing sugar, for dusting

Preparation time: 10 minutes, plus cooling and standing
Cooking time: about 1 hour
Oven: 160°C, 325°F, Gas Mark 3

1. Place the bran and sultanas in a small bowl and pour over the orange juice. Leave to stand for 30 minutes.
2. Sift the flour and cocoa into a mixing bowl and rub in the margarine until the mixture resembles fine breadcrumbs.
3. Stir in the sugar, nuts, nutmeg, bran mixture and eggs to produce a stiff dough.
4. Spoon the mixture into a greased 450 g (1 lb) loaf tin and bake in a preheated oven until well risen, golden and firm to the touch. Turn out and cool on a wire tray.
5. To make the filling, if using, beat the cheese until smooth. Melt the chocolate in a heatproof bowl set over a pan of hot water and stir until melted. Beat the chocolate into the cheese.
6. Split the loaf into 2 layers, sandwich with half the filling and top with the remainder. Decorate with walnut halves, lightly dusted with icing sugar.

CHOCOLATE VICTORIA SANDWICH

Makes one 20 cm (8 inch) cake
225 g (8 oz) butter or block margarine
225 g (8 oz) caster sugar
4 eggs
200 g (7 oz) self-raising flour
50 g (2 oz) cocoa
1 tablespoon warm water

Preparation time: 15-20 minutes, plus cooling
Cooking time: 25-30 minutes
Oven: 180°C, 350°F, Gas Mark 4

1. Grease two 20 cm (8 inch) deep-sided sandwich tins and line with greaseproof paper.
2. Cream the butter or margarine and caster sugar until very light and fluffy. The mixture should resemble the consistency of fresh whipped cream.
3. Add the eggs one at a time, beating well between each addition. If the mixture appears to curdle, beat in 1 tablespoon of the flour before the last egg.
4. Sift the flour and cocoa together. With a metal spoon, fold half into the creamed mixture. When thoroughly incorporated, lightly fold in the remaining flour mixture and the water.
5. Divide the mixture between the prepared tins and spread evenly. Bake in a preheated oven for 25-30 minutes until the cakes are well risen and brown and spring back when lightly pressed with a finger. Turn out on a wire tray to cool. ⑤
6. When cold, fill as desired.

⑤ Open freeze, then wrap in cling film. Thaw unwrapped.

CHOCOLATE BUTTER CREAM

Will fill and coat the top of one 20 cm (8 inch) Victoria sandwich
2 tablespoons cocoa
2 tablespoons boiling water
100 g (4 oz) butter
225 g (8 oz) icing sugar

Preparation time: 15 minutes

1. Blend the cocoa with the boiling water.
2. Cream the butter and half the sugar until light and fluffy.
3. Gradually work in the remaining sugar, then beat in the cocoa paste.

PARTY TIME

CHOC 'N' NUT SQUARES

Makes about 20 squares
175 g (6 oz) plain flour
2 tablespoons cocoa
75 g (3 oz) instant custard powder
175 g (6 oz) butter or block margarine
75 g (3 oz) caster sugar
Topping:
75 g (3 oz) butter
75 g (3 oz) dark brown sugar
1 tablespoon clear or set honey
100 g (4 oz) nuts, chopped and toasted
100 g (4 oz) dipping, plain or milk cooking chocolate,
   broken into pieces (optional)

Preparation time: 20 minutes, plus cooling
Cooking time: 1-1½ hours
Oven: 150°C, 300°F, Gas Mark 2

1. Sieve the flour and cocoa into a large mixing bowl. Add the custard powder, then rub the butter or margarine into the mixture until it begins to become sticky.
2. Add the caster sugar and continue rubbing until the mixture begins to form a solid mass. Press into a ball shape and knead lightly with a little extra flour until smooth.
3. Line the base of an 18 cm (7 inch) square cake tin with a piece of greased greaseproof paper. Press the dough into the base of the cake tin to cover it, pushing well into the corners. Prick the surface with a fork.
4. Bake in a preheated oven for 1¼-1½ hours until the mixture begins to brown. Cool in the tin for 10 minutes then carefully turn out. Peel off the paper and cool on a wire tray.
5. Melt the butter, sugar and honey in a small heavy-based saucepan, over a low heat. Once melted, boil for 3 minutes, stirring constantly. Away from the heat, stir in the nuts and spread the mixture over the biscuit base. Leave to set for about 15 minutes.
6. Cut the biscuit slab into about 20 equal squares then leave them to set firmly, about 30 minutes.
7. If liked, place the chocolate in a small heatproof bowl and set over a pan of hot water until melted. Dip the top of each square diagonally into the chocolate and place on waxed or non-stick silicone paper to set.

VARIETY SQUARES

rice paper
225 g (8 oz) granulated sugar
225 g (8 oz) soft brown sugar
150 ml (¼ pint) water
2 egg whites
100 g (4 oz) desiccated coconut, toasted
100 g (4 oz) glacé cherries, quartered
25 g (1 oz) angelica, chopped (optional)
100 g (4 oz) dipping or cooking chocolate

Preparation time: 20 minutes, plus cooling and setting
Cooking time: about 10 minutes

1. Dampen the inside of a 20×20 cm (8×8 inch) square cake tin. Line the base with a sheet of rice paper.
2. In a heavy-based saucepan, heat the sugars and water very gently until dissolved, then boil to the soft crack stage on a sugar thermometer, 132°C-142°C, 270°F-286°F. Alternatively, drop a little syrup into iced water. Remove from the water and gently stretch it between the fingers. It should form hard but elastic strands and only feel slightly sticky.
3. Whisk the egg whites until stiff, then gradually beat in the syrup. When the mixture becomes very stiff add the coconut, glacé cherries and angelica, if using. Mix well, then pour into the tin. Cover with more rice paper and press down with a heavy weight.
4. Leave the nougat to stand or chill for at least 24 hours then ease out of the tin and cut into squares.
5. Melt the chocolate in a small heatproof bowl set over a pan of hot water. Stir until smooth.
6. Carefully dip each piece of nougat into the chocolate so that only half the square is covered. Cool until set on waxed or greaseproof paper.

TOP: Choc 'n' nut squares BOTTOM: Variety squares

TOP: Chocolate stars; Caramel crunch biscuits BOTTOM: Chocolate fudge

CHOCOLATE FUDGE

Makes 50-60 pieces
50 g (2 oz) butter, plus extra for greasing
100 g (4 oz) plain chocolate, broken into pieces
5 tablespoons evaporated milk
1 teaspoon vanilla essence
450 g (1 lb) icing sugar, sieved
50 g (2 oz) chopped nuts, toasted (optional)
100 g (4 oz) plain chocolate, broken into pieces, to decorate

Preparation time: 15 minutes, plus cooling
Cooking time: about 5 minutes

1. Grease an 18-20 cm (7-8 inch) square tin with butter.
2. Place the butter, chocolate and evaporated milk in a small heatproof bowl set over a pan of hot water. Stir vigorously until smooth. Add the vanilla essence.
3. Pour the chocolate mixture into the icing sugar and nuts, if using. Beat until thoroughly blended.
4. Press into the greased tin and leave in a cool place to set.
5. When cool, melt the chocolate for decoration in a heatproof bowl set over a bowl of hot water. Stir until smooth. Spread over the fudge with a spatula. Roughen the surface with a fork and leave until set.
6. Cut the fudge into squares. Store in an airtight container for 3-4 days.

Variations:
Use milk or white chocolate for a milder chocolate flavour, and replace the nuts with an equal quantity of chopped glacé cherries and chopped angelica.

CHOCOLATE STARS

100 g (4 oz) butter or block margarine,
    plus extra for greasing
200 g (7 oz) plain flour
25 g (1 oz) cornflour
75 g (3 oz) caster sugar
25 g (1 oz) drinking chocolate powder
grated rind of 1 orange
1 egg
Icing:
450 g (1 lb) icing sugar, sifted
4 tablespoons orange juice
a little orange food colouring
2 tablespoons cocoa, sifted
2 tablespoons boiling water

Preparation time: about 1 hour, plus cooling
Cooking time: 30 minutes
Oven: 180°C, 350°F, Gas Mark 4

1. Rub the fat into the sifted flour and cornflour then add the sugar, drinking chocolate powder and orange rind. Stir well then add the egg. Mix to a smooth dough.
2. Lightly knead the dough and roll out on a floured work surface to about 5 mm (¼ inch) thick. Cut out star shapes using a cutter or cardboard template about 7.5 cm (3 inches) in diameter (from point to point).
3. Bake in 2 batches on 2 greased baking sheets in a preheated oven for about 15 minutes, until firm and golden brown. Cool on a wire tray.
4. To make the icing, blend the icing sugar with the orange juice. Spoon 3 tablespoons of the icing into a cup and mix with a little orange colouring, adding a little more icing sugar if necessary, to make a smooth piping consistency.
5. Spoon the orange icing into a small greaseproof paper icing bag and cut a very small hole to produce a fine line when piped.
6. Blend the cocoa with the boiling water, cool slightly, then mix with the remaining icing, adding a little more icing sugar, if necessary, to make a stiff coating consistency.
7. Coat the top surface of 2-3 biscuits at a time with the chocolate icing and while wet, pipe about 4-5 circles of orange icing starting in the centre.
8. With a fine skewer, draw the icing from the centre outwards to each point, then draw inwards from the angle at the base of each point to the centre. Repeat until all the biscuits are coated. Leave to dry.

CARAMEL CRUNCH BISCUITS

Makes 24 squares
butter or margarine, melted, for greasing
100 g (4 oz) butter or block margarine
25 g (1 oz) caster sugar
25 g (1 oz) drinking chocolate powder
1 teaspoon vanilla essence
175 g (6 oz) digestive biscuits, crushed
50 g (2 oz) chopped nuts (unsalted peanuts, hazelnuts,
    almonds, walnuts)
2nd layer:
1 × 400 g (14 oz) can condensed milk
25 g (1 oz) butter
3 tablespoons golden syrup
1 teaspoon vanilla essence
3rd layer:
100 g (4 oz) plain or milk chocolate

Preparation time: 30 minutes, plus chilling
Cooking time: about 8 minutes

If using a non-stick Swiss roll tin, line the base with greased greaseproof paper.

1. Brush an 18 × 28 cm (7 × 11 inch) Swiss roll tin with the melted fat.
2. To make the first layer, melt the butter or margarine, sugar, chocolate powder and vanilla essence in a saucepan over low heat. Stir well.
3. Stir the crushed biscuits and chopped nuts into the melted mixture until all the fat has been absorbed. Press the mixture into the bottom of the Swiss roll tin.
4. Tip all the second layer ingredients into a small heavy-based saucepan and heat gently until the mixture begins to bubble. Stir vigorously and continuously while the mixture boils gently for 3 minutes. A brown skin will form on the sides of the pan and this should be stirred in vigorously. Avoid allowing the mixture to burn.
5. Pour the caramel mixture over the biscuit base and spread evenly with a palette knife.
6. Place the chocolate in a small heatproof bowl and set the bowl over a pan of hot water. Stir until melted.
7. Pour the chocolate over the caramel. Spread evenly and mark a pattern with the blunt side of a knife. Chill until set, about 2 hours.
8. Mark the chocolate into 24 equal squares. Cut in the tin using a sharp knife and lift each square out with a palette knife.

MUSHROOM CAKE

½ quantity Chocolate victoria sandwich mixture
  (page 51)
1 quantity Chocolate butter cream (page 51)
225 g (8 oz) marzipan
2 tablespoons seedless jam, warmed
icing sugar, to dust

Preparation time: 25 minutes
Cooking time: 25-30 minutes
Oven: 180°C, 350°F, Gas Mark 4

1. Bake the Victoria sandwich mixture in one 20 cm (8 inch) deep-sided sandwich tin, as directed on page 51. Turn out and cool on a wire tray.
2. Using a piping bag fitted with a large star, cake decorating nozzle, pipe lines of butter cream from the edge of the cake to the centre until the whole top is covered.
3. Reserve 25 g (1 oz) of the marzipan and roll the remainder into a sausage about 60 cm (24 inches) long, then roll a thin strip that will cover and just stand above the cake sides.
4. Brush the side of the cake with the jam and press the strip on top. Roll a clean, straight-sided jar several times over the join to blend it together. Push the marzipan above the level of the side inwards so that it curves slightly over the piped ridges.
5. Shape the remaining marzipan into a 'stalk' and place in the centre. Dust the cake lightly with icing sugar.

Variation:
CHOCOLATE BUTTERFLIES
Divide the cake mixture between about 14-16 paper cases and bake in a preheated oven set at 190°C, 375°F, Gas Mark 5 for about 15-20 minutes, until well risen. When cold, cut a circle from the top of each, using a sharp knife. Cut each small circle in half. Spoon or pipe a little butter cream into the centre of each cake, using a star nozzle, and press two semi-circular pieces into it to look like butterfly wings. Dust with icing sugar and top with a halved glacé cherry, nuts or chocolate vermicelli.

> To measure the marzipan for the cake exactly, cut 2 pieces of string, one 5 mm (¼ inch) higher than the cake, and the other the exact width around the cake. Roll out the marzipan and trim length and width to the size of the string. Roll the marzipan into a coil and place one end on the side of the cake. Unroll carefully around the cake to cover it evenly. Use a jam jar or small palette knife to smooth the join.

CHOCOLATE FINGER DIPS

Serves 6-8
200 g (7 oz) plain flour
25 g (1 oz) caster sugar
25 g (1 oz) ground semolina
25 g (1 oz) hazelnuts, finely ground (optional)
grated rind of 1 lemon
100 g (4 oz) butter or margarine
1 egg
Dip:
200 g (7 oz) milk chocolate, broken into pieces
25 g (1 oz) butter
100 ml (4 fl oz) milk, warmed
25 g (1 oz) hazelnuts, finely ground and toasted

Preparation time: 15 minutes, plus cooling
Cooking time: 10-15 minutes
Oven: 180°C, 350°F, Gas Mark 4

1. Combine the flour, sugar, semolina, hazelnuts, if using, and lemon rind in a mixing bowl and rub in the fat until the mixture resembles fine breadcrumbs. Add the egg and mix to a soft pliable dough. Knead lightly on a floured work surface until smooth.
2. Roll out the dough into a rectangle 20×25 cm (8× 10 inches) and 5 mm (¼ inch) thick. Cut the rectangle in half across its short width, then cut each small rectangle into sticks or fingers of dough about 1 cm (½ inch) wide.
3. Transfer to 2 greased baking sheets and bake in a preheated oven for 10-15 minutes until golden in colour. Lift on to a wire tray to cool. Ⓐ
4. To make the Dip, melt the chocolate in a small heatproof bowl over a saucepan of hot water. Add the butter and stir vigorously until thick and smooth.
5. Gradually add the warmed milk, beating well between each addition until the dip is smooth and runny. Stir in the nuts if using.
6. Divide the dip between 6-8 individual patterned waxed paper cups or pour into a small bowl, and leave until cold, about 1 hour. The dip will thicken on cooling. Ⓐ
7. Divide the cooled biscuits into 6-8 equal bundles and wrap each with a napkin that matches the waxed paper cups.

Ⓐ Can be made 2-3 days in advance and stored in an airtight container.
Ⓐ Can be made the day before. Keep covered and chill.

LEFT TO RIGHT: Mushroom cake; Chocolate finger dips; Surprise cones

SURPRISE CONES

Makes 10

10 round ice cream cones
50 g (2 oz) unsalted mixed nuts, chopped and toasted
10 pink and white marshmallows
icing sugar, for tossing
200 g (7 oz) milk chocolate, broken into pieces
4 tablespoons milk or evaporated milk, warmed
25 g (1 oz) chocolate vermicelli or hundreds and thousands, to decorate

Preparation time: 25 minutes, plus cooling

1. Prop up the ends of a wire tray so that the cones can sit upright, stuck into the tray.

2. Sprinkle a few nuts in the bottom of each cone.

3. Snip the marshmallows roughly into small pieces with kitchen scissors and toss in a little icing sugar to keep the pieces separate. Mix with the nuts.

4. Melt the chocolate in a small heatproof bowl set over a saucepan of hot water. When smooth, beat in the warmed milk or evaporated milk a little at a time, until smooth. Leave until cool but still soft, about 30 minutes.

5. Stir the marshmallows and nuts into the chocolate mixture and leave until completely cold, but still sticky, about 1 hour.

6. Just before serving, place about 2 heaped teaspoons of the chocolate mixture in the cone and round the top.

7. Dip the top of each cone into the chocolate vermicelli or hundreds and thousands and serve immediately, before the cones start to soften.

LEFT TO RIGHT: Marble cake; Chocolate fudge bars; Peanut cookies

MARBLE CAKE

Serves 8-10

175 g (6 oz) butter, plus extra for greasing
175 g (6 oz) caster sugar
3 eggs
225 g (8 oz) self-raising flour
2 tablespoons cocoa
2 teaspoons coffee powder or granules
2 tablespoons hot water
½ teaspoon vanilla essence
½ teaspoon peppermint essence
a little green food colouring
icing sugar, for dusting

Preparation time: 20 minutes, plus cooling
Cooking time: 40-45 minutes
Oven: 180°C, 350°F, Gas Mark 4

1. Grease a 1.5 litre (2½ pint) ring mould with butter.
2. Cream the butter and sugar until it is very light and fluffy and has the appearance of fresh whipped cream.
3. Beat in the eggs, one at a time, and if the mixture looks as if it may curdle, beat in 1 tablespoon of the flour before the last egg.
4. Sift the flour over the mixture and fold lightly but thoroughly until evenly mixed.
5. Divide the mixture into 3 separate mixing bowls. Blend the cocoa and coffee with the hot water. When cool, beat into one lot of mixture.
6. Beat the vanilla essence into the second lot of mixture, and the mint flavouring, to taste, and green food colouring into the third.
7. Spoon the mixtures alternately, one heaped table-spoon at a time, into the prepared ring mould until it has all been used up. Draw a fine skewer through the mixture right round the ring mould, twice, to blend the colours slightly.
8. Bake in a preheated oven for 40-45 minutes until the cake is well risen and springs back when lightly pressed with the finger. Turn out and cool on a wire tray.
9. When cold, dust lightly with icing sugar.

CHOCOLATE FUDGE BARS

Makes 15-20
4 tablespoons golden syrup
100 g (4 oz) butter or block margarine
100 g (4 oz) plain cooking chocolate or cake covering, broken into pieces
225 g (8 oz) digestive or other unfilled or coated sweet biscuits, coarsely crushed
50 g (2 oz) shredded coconut or chopped nuts
50 g (2 oz) glacé cherries, quartered
50 g (2 oz) sultanas

Preparation time: about 15 minutes

1. Spoon the syrup into a heavy-based saucepan and add the butter or margarine. Heat gently until both are melted and stir well.
2. Away from the heat, add the chocolate and stir vigorously until well blended.
3. Stir the biscuit crumbs, nuts, cherries and sultanas into the chocolate mixture. Mix well.
4. Line the base of an 18 cm (7 inch) square cake tin with greased greaseproof paper. Pour in the mixture, spread evenly and press down firmly. Cool, then chill until set, about 3 hours.
5. Carefully turn out the fudge biscuit slab on to a chopping board and cut into approximately 15 bars. Keep chilled in warm weather.

PEANUT COOKIES

Makes 24 squares
25 rectangular ice cream wafers
175 g (6 oz) plain chocolate, broken into pieces
40 g (1½ oz) butter
3 tablespoons golden syrup
1 × 400 g (14 oz) can condensed milk
4 tablespoons crunchy peanut butter

Preparation time: 20 minutes, plus chilling
Cooking time: about 5 minutes

1. Line the base of a 28 × 18 cm (11 × 7 inch) Swiss roll tin with foil. Line the base of the tin with the ice cream wafers and trim where necessary to fit perfectly. Remove the wafers from the tin, then fit and trim the remaining wafers in the same way. Lift out and keep the 2 lots separate. Brush any crumbs out of the tin.
2. Melt the chocolate and 15 g (½ oz) of the butter in a small heatproof bowl set over a saucepan of hot water. Stir vigorously until smooth.
3. Spread half the chocolate over the base of the foil-lined tin and cover with a layer of the wafers.
4. Melt the remaining butter, golden syrup and condensed milk in a heavy-based saucepan. Heat gently until the mixture begins to bubble. Stir vigorously while the mixture boils for 3 minutes. Away from the heat, beat in the peanut butter. Continue beating until very thick, then spoon on to the wafer layer in the tin and smooth level.
5. Fit the remaining wafers over the fudge filling, pressing them down well, and spread the rest of the chocolate on top.
6. Chill for about 30 minutes until the chocolate has set. With a sharp knife, cut into 24 squares. Lift out of the tin and carefully peel off the foil.

CHOCOLATE COCONUT PYRAMIDS

Makes 30
1×383 g (13½ oz) can condensed milk
350 g (12 oz) unsweetened desiccated coconut
25 g (1 oz) drinking chocolate powder
50 g (2 oz) chocolate drops for cooking
2 large sheets rice paper or non-stick silicone paper
To decorate: (optional)
75 g (3 oz) plain or milk cooking chocolate,
  broken into pieces
25 g (1 oz) desiccated or shredded coconut
about 7 glacé cherries, quartered

Preparation time: 15 minutes, plus cooling
Cooking time: about 15-20 minutes
Oven: 190°C, 375°F, Gas Mark 5

1. Pour the condensed milk into a large mixing bowl with the desiccated coconut, chocolate powder and chocolate drops. Beat well until thoroughly mixed.
2. Line 2 large baking sheets with the rice paper and spoon the coconut mixture into 30 mounds, about 2 heaped teaspoons of mixture to each mound. Leave a gap between each one as the mixture spreads a little during cooking.
3. Bake in a preheated oven for about 15-20 minutes until tinged brown all over. The mixture will still feel soft to press and will harden on cooling.
4. Lift the pyramids on to a wire tray to cool, roughly tearing the rice paper between them. Tear the paper away neatly when cold. Or lift the pyramids off the silicone paper on to a wire tray to cool. Ⓐ
5. Place the chocolate, if using, in a small heatproof bowl and set over a pan of hot water until melted. Stir well until smooth.
6. Swirl a little melted chocolate on the top of each pyramid, sprinkle over a little coconut and top with a quartered glacé cherry. Leave to set, about 30 minutes.

Ⓐ Can be made 2-3 days in advance. Store in an airtight tin.

> Treasure cups can also be used to serve individual helpings of Chocolate fudge ice cream (page 13). For an elegant finale to a dinner party, serve the Treasure cups filled with a rich chocolate mousse, such as the Iced rum and raisin mousse (page 32) and finished off with a swirl of whipped cream.

CHOCOLATE TREASURE CUPS

175-225 g (6-8 oz) dipping, plain or cake covering chocolate
6 teaspoons strawberry or raspberry jam
3 trifle sponge cakes
1×300 g (11 oz) can mandarin orange segments in natural
  juice, drained and juice reserved
2 teaspoons powdered gelatine
100 g (4 oz) red glacé cherries, or
  red, green and yellow mixed, washed and dried

Preparation time: 35 minutes, plus setting

1. Line a tray or baking sheet with greaseproof paper. Melt the chocolate in a small heatproof bowl set over a pan of hot water.
2. Using a teaspoon, spread enough chocolate into 6 individual aluminium foil cases 7.5 cm (3 inches) in diameter and 5-6 cm (2-2½ inches) deep to coat the insides evenly. Once coated, invert each case on to the greaseproof paper and leave until the chocolate is firm, about 20 minutes. Keep the remaining chocolate liquid over hot water.
3. When the chocolate-lined cases are firm, repeat the coating layer with the remaining chocolate and invert on the greaseproof paper. Leave until set hard, about 1 hour.
4. When hard, turn each case the right way up. Place 1 teaspoon of jam in each one. Break the trifle sponges into small pieces and place in a bowl.
5. Divide the mandarin segments into 2 portions and roughly chop them, cutting each segment into about 4 pieces. Combine one portion with the sponge cake.
6. Pour the juice into a small saucepan and sprinkle over the gelatine. Heat gently without boiling until dissolved. Pour the juice over the sponge cake and stir well. Cool.
7. Spoon the sponge mixture into the chocolate cases. Smooth level, then chill until set, about 1 hour. Release the filled chocolate cases from the foil containers by gently running your thumbnail between the chocolate and the case. Alternatively, carefully release the cups with a round-bladed knife.
8. Roughly chop the glacé cherries, then wash and dry on paper towels. Spoon the reserved chopped mandarin segments over the cups (if liked) and sprinkle with the chopped cherries.

CHOCOLATE HONEY TOFFEE

Makes about 36 squares
100 g (4 oz) butter, plus extra for greasing
225 g (8 oz) clear or set honey
50 g (2 oz) soft brown sugar
2 teaspoons ground cinnamon
75 g (3 oz) dipping or cooking chocolate

Preparation time: 10 minutes, plus cooling
Cooking time: 15 minutes

1. Grease an 18-20 cm (7-8 inch) square tin with butter.
2. Place the honey and sugar in a heavy-based saucepan and heat gently, stirring constantly, until the sugar dissolves.
3. Add the butter and stir until melted. Boil the mixture until the soft crack stage is reached on a sugar thermometer, 132°C-142°C, 270°C-286°F. Alternatively, drop a little of the toffee into iced water. Remove from the water and gently stretch it between the fingers. It should form hard but elastic strands, and only feel slightly sticky.
4. Away from the heat, sprinkle in the cinnamon and beat thoroughly, then pour into the prepared tin. Leave in a cool place until almost firm but still slightly soft, then mark it into squares with a knife. When cold, break into squares.
5. Melt the chocolate in a small heatproof bowl set over a saucepan of hot water. Stir until melted, then dip half each piece of toffee into the chocolate. Leave the toffee on waxed paper or non-stick silicone paper until set.

LEFT: Chocolate coconut pyramids RIGHT: Chocolate honey toffee; Chocolate treasure cups

WILLIE WASP

butter or margarine, for greasing
1 quantity Quick chocolate cake mix (page 66)
1 quantity Chocolate butter cream (page 51)
about 25 g (1 oz) chocolate vermicelli
350 g (12 oz) yellow marzipan
3 tablespoons cocoa
2 tablespoons boiling water
icing sugar, for kneading
175 g (6 oz) white chocolate
25 g (1 oz) plain cooking chocolate (optional)

Preparation time: 45 minutes, plus cooling
Cooking time: 45 minutes
Oven: 160°C, 325°F, Gas Mark 3

1. Grease a 600 ml (1 pint) pudding basin and line the base with a disc of greaseproof paper. Grease a 450 g (1 lb) loaf tin measuring about 9×19×5 cm (3½×7½×2 inches). Fill both containers two-thirds full with the cake mixture. Smooth level.
2. Bake in a preheated oven for 45 minutes or until the cakes are well risen and spring back when lightly pressed with the finger. Turn out and cool on a wire rack.
3. Cut the loaf along its length and sandwich together with a little butter cream. Place diagonally on a 25 cm (10 inch) cake board.
4. Flat base down, cut the pudding cake from top to bottom into two-thirds and one-third. Use butter cream to sandwich the cut edge of the large piece against one end of the loaf, and the smaller piece against the other. Trim the sides level with the loaf cake.
5. Reserve 2 tablespoons of butter cream and cover the cake with the remainder. Coat the large rounded end with the vermicelli to represent the head.
6. Divide the marzipan into 150 g (5 oz) and 200 g (7 oz) portions. Blend the cocoa with the water, then cool. Mix the cocoa into the 200 g (7 oz) marzipan and knead with icing sugar until smooth.
7. Roll 2 small balls of the yellow marzipan to make eyes and a fine strip for a mouth. Roll the remainder into a rectangle 10×20 cm (4×8 inches). Roll 100 g (4 oz) of the chocolate marzipan into a rectangle 7.5× 2 cm (3×8 inches). Cut each rectangle into four and three 2.5×20 cm (1×8 inch) strips respectively. Lay these bands alternately from the head join, beginning and ending with a yellow band.
8. Mould 50 g (2 oz) of the remaining chocolate marzipan over the small rounded end, so the body is covered. Tuck the uneven edge under the last yellow band. Brush the marzipan body with a little water.
9. Half cover 2 cocktail sticks with a little of the remaining marzipan and place a small ball on each to represent antennae. Push into the head.

10. Fix the eyes and mouth in place with butter cream.
11. Roll the remaining chocolate marzipan into a long sausage and cut into six 15 cm (6 inch) lengths. Dab a little butter icing on each end. Stick one end on to the body and bend the leg, sticking the other end on to the cake board. Repeat with all the legs.
12. Melt the white chocolate over a pan of hot water. Draw two wing shapes about 18 cm (7 inches) long and 7.5 cm (3 inches) wide on greaseproof paper. Spread the melted chocolate on the paper. Cool until set.
13. If liked, melt the plain chocolate, fill a small greaseproof paper icing bag and pipe fine lines on the wing shapes to look like veins. Cool until set, then lift off the paper.
14. With a sharp knife, cut a line lengthways either side of the top of the striped body. Open slightly with the knife and gently push in the wings. Keep chilled in warm weather.

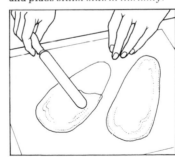

1. Place the loaf cake diagonally on the board. Divide the pudding cake and place either side of the body.

2. Lay alternate strips of yellow and chocolate marzipan over the body, from the head join.

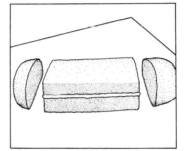

3. Spread melted white chocolate on greaseproof paper to make the wing shapes.

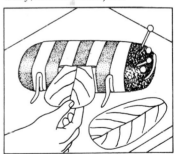

4. Make slits either side of the striped body, then gently push in the wing shapes.

OZZY OWL

1 quantity Quick chocolate cake mix (page 66)
1 quantity Chocolate butter cream (page 51)
1 round ice cream cone
150 g (5 oz) marzipan
brown food colouring
25 g (1 oz) white chocolate
225 g (8 oz) dark chocolate buttons

Preparation time: 45 minutes, plus cooling
Cooking time: about 1¼ hours
Oven: 160°C, 325°F, Gas Mark 3

If you do not have brown food colouring, mix a little red and green colouring to make brown. It is important to use a true scarlet red and not cochineal.

1. Prepare and cool the cake mixture as for Thomas toad (right) up to and including step 4. Stand the cakes on a circular serving dish or cake board. Reserve about 3 tablespoons of the butter cream and use the rest to cover the cakes completely. Stand on a round cake board or plate.
2. Cut the ice cream cone about 5 cm (2 inches) from the tip and discard the tip end. Cut the remainder of the cone in half along its length and with a sharp knife trim each thin end of the cone to a point to make ears. Cover with some butter cream and stick on top of the cakes.
3. Divide the marzipan into 75 g (3 oz) and 50 g (2 oz) pieces. Colour the small piece brown and use about a quarter to shape into a small hooked beak. Make 2 claws with 3 toes on each with the remainder.
4. Halve the yellow marzipan, knead until smooth, then shape into 2 thick ovals to form wings. Press these on to either side of the lower body and curve them away from the body at the top so there is a small hollow space between the wing and the body. Cover with the remaining butter cream.
5. Melt the white chocolate in a small heatproof bowl set over a pan of hot water. Stir until smooth. Draw 2 oval shapes on greaseproof paper about the size of a large egg. Spread the chocolate in the ovals and place a chocolate button in each to make eyes. Make sure the buttons are in the same position so that the eyes look in the same direction. Cool until set.
6. Place a row of chocolate buttons around the base of the owl, then place another row above so the buttons just overlap. Continue with the rows of buttons until the whole owl is covered, just leaving the face free.
7. Carefully lift the eyes off the paper and press into place. Position the beak and claws.

THOMAS TOAD

1 quantity Quick chocolate cake mix (page 66)
1 quantity Chocolate butter cream (page 51)
50 g (2 oz) chocolate vermicelli
2 chocolate dome-shaped marshmallow cakes
25 g (1 oz) desiccated coconut
blue food colouring
100 g (4 oz) yellow marzipan
red food colouring
green food colouring
a little icing sugar

Preparation time: 45 minutes, plus cooling
Cooking time: about 45 minutes-1¼ hours
Oven: 160°C, 325°F, Gas Mark 3

1. Grease one 600 ml (1 pint) and one 900 ml (1½ pint) pudding basin and cut 2 discs of greaseproof paper to line the base of each. Two-thirds fill each basin with the cake mixture.
2. Bake the small cake in a preheated oven for about 45 minutes, and the large one for 1¼ hours, until they are well risen and spring back when pressed with the finger. Turn out, remove the paper and cool on a wire rack.
3. Slice both cakes in half horizontally and sandwich back together with a little butter cream.
4. Place the large cake, flat side down, on a cake board and sandwich the small one (flat side down) on top with butter cream.
5. Reserve one tablespoon of butter cream and coat the cakes with the rest. Cover with chocolate vermicelli.
6. Use the reserved butter cream to stick the marshmallow cakes on top at a slight angle to make eyes.
7. With a sharp knife, make a slit about halfway down the side of the top cake, underneath the eyes, to make a mouth. Make the cut deep, slanting down to the bottom of the cake, so that the mouth will open gently. Secure the open mouth with a cocktail stick.
8. Mix the coconut with a little blue food colouring and spread over the cake board around the toad.
9. Divide the marzipan into two-thirds and a third. Colour the large portion green. Halve the small portion, and colour one piece red.
10. Mould the red piece to rest in the base of the mouth. Shape 9 discs with the green marzipan and place in groups of 3 around the toad to represent leaves. Shape 3 small thick discs with the yellow marzipan and using scissors snip small triangles out of the edge of the discs to look like water lilies. Close up slightly and position on the leaves.
11. Make up a little thick white icing with some icing sugar and water. Dab a little on both eyes and in the centre of each water lily.

TOP: Ozzy owl BOTTOM: Chocolate pond; Thomas toad

CHOCOLATE POND

Serves 6-8

50 ml (2 fl oz) double cream, whipped
about 12 miniature chocolate eggs, unwrapped
1 × 150 g (5 oz) lime jelly, set in a large shallow dish
coloured sugar flowers
50 g (2 oz) strip of angelica

Preparation time: 20 minutes, plus setting

1. Fill a cake decorating bag fitted with a fine writing nozzle with the cream and pipe blobs for eyes and a mouth on the one end of each egg. Stick on to the lime jelly with a large blob of cream.
2. Stick coloured sugar flowers in groups on the jelly.
3. Cut the angelica into fine strips and pierce into the jelly to look like reeds. Chill before serving.

Variation:
Use chocolate creme filled eggs. Stick halved glacé cherries on for eyes, and chocolate buttons for feet.

Choc around the clock; Meringue shapes

QUICK CHOCOLATE CAKE MIX

**Makes one 20 cm (8 inch) round or
one 18 cm (7 inch) square cake**
200 g (7 oz) self-raising flour
25 g (1 oz) cocoa
225 g (8 oz) soft margarine
225 g (8 oz) caster sugar
4 eggs

**Preparation time: 5 minutes
Cooking time: 25-30 minutes
Oven: 180°C, 350°F, Gas Mark 4**

1. Sift the flour and cocoa into a mixing bowl and add the margarine, sugar and eggs.
2. Beat thoroughly with a wooden spoon until the mixture is smooth and blended.
3. Divide the mixture between two greased 20 cm (8 inch) deep-sided round tins, or two 18 cm (7 inch) square sandwich tins. Smooth level with a spatula.
4. Bake in a preheated oven for 25-30 minutes until the cake is well risen and springs back when pressed lightly with a finger. Turn out the cake on to a wire tray and cool.

MERINGUE SHAPES

Makes 6 animal shapes or rosettes and stars
4 egg whites
100 g (4 oz) caster sugar
100 g (4 oz) icing sugar
25 g (1 oz) cocoa
To decorate:
36 whole cloves
12 flaked almonds
6 pieces of string (optional)
50 g (2 oz) slivered almonds
225 g (8 oz) dipping or cooking chocolate (optional)

Preparation time: 45 minutes
Cooking time: 45 minutes - 1 hour
Oven: 150°C, 350°F, Gas Mark 2

1. Whisk the egg whites until standing in stiff peaks. Add the caster sugar, then whisk again until the meringue is glossy and standing in very stiff peaks. Fold in the icing sugar and cocoa. Line baking sheets with non-stick silicone paper.
2. SNAILS: Using a 1 cm (½ inch) plain nozzle, pipe a short straight length of meringue to form a head, then bring the straight line out to make a circle, and continue piping in a spiral to form the shell. Stick two whole cloves in the head to make feelers.
MICE: Using a 1 cm (½ inch) plain nozzle, pipe forward about 2.5 cm (1 inch), then pipe a large bulb of meringue back over this, releasing pressure into a long-drawn-out point. Push 2 whole cloves right into the meringue to form eyes at the pointed end, flaked almonds for ears and a short piece of string for a tail.
HEDGEHOGS: Using a 2 cm (¾ inch) star nozzle, pipe forward about 2.5 cm (1 inch) then pipe back over this, releasing pressure to form a short point. Push 2 whole cloves into the pointed end of the meringue to form eyes and push halved slivered almonds all over the back to form the spines.
STARS: Using a 2 cm (¾ inch) star nozzle, hold the bag vertically and push out a star of icing. Release pressure quickly to avoid a long point.
ROSETTES: Using a 2 cm (¾ inch) star nozzle, pipe a small circle of meringue then finish by bringing the nozzle into the centre of the circle. Release quickly.
3. Bake the meringues in a preheated oven for about 45 minutes to 1 hour, depending on size. They should be completely dried out. Cool on a wire tray. Ⓐ
4. If liked, prepare some dipping chocolate and dip the shells of the snails, the backs of the mice and hedgehogs and spirals and the tip or base of the rosettes and stars in the chocolate. Dry on waxed or greaseproof paper.

Ⓐ The meringue shapes can be stored, uncoated, for up to 3 weeks in an airtight container.

CHOC AROUND THE CLOCK

275 g (10 oz) self-raising flour
25 g (1 oz) cornflour
50 g (2 oz) cocoa
pinch of salt
275 g (10 oz) caster sugar
4 eggs, separated
200 ml (7 fl oz) corn oil
200 ml (7 fl oz) water
butter or margarine, for greasing
To decorate:
1 quantity Chocolate butter cream (page 51)
about 52 chocolate finger biscuits
100 g (4 oz) icing sugar
1 tablespoon water
2 round chocolate marshmallow cakes (optional)

Preparation time: 30 minutes, plus cooling
Cooking time: 25-30 minutes
Oven: 190°C, 375°F, Gas Mark 5

1. Sieve the dry ingredients into a bowl and stir in the egg yolks, oil and water. Beat lightly with a wooden spoon to form a smooth batter.
2. Whisk the eggs until standing in stiff peaks and fold lightly into the batter.
3. Pour the cake mixture into 3 greased 18 cm (7 inch) square sandwich tins and bake in a preheated oven for 25-30 minutes, until well risen and springy when lightly pressed with the finger. Turn out and cool on a wire tray.
4. Reserve 4 tablespoons of the butter cream and sandwich the cakes together with half the remainder. Smoothly coat the sides with the rest, and place to one end of a 35.5 cm (14 inch) square cake board.
5. Stick the chocolate finger biscuits all the way round.
6. Mark out a circle with a knife about 15 cm (6 inches) in diameter on top of the cake, using a saucer as a guide.
7. Fill a small piping bag fitted with a medium star nozzle with 3 tablespoons of the butter cream. Pipe stars to fill the area outside the circle.
8. Mix the icing sugar with the water to a thick consistency and spread in the circle. Leave until set.
9. Fill a small greaseproof paper decorating bag (page 9) with the remaining butter cream and pipe the clock numbers and hands on the circle.
10. If liked, pipe 2 chains of tiny circles below the clock on the board, one shorter than the other and place the marshmallow cakes on the end.

ROUND THE WORLD

AUSTRALIA

CHOCOLATE PAVLOVA

Serves 4-6
3 egg whites
225 g (8 oz) caster sugar
25 g (1 oz) cornflour
25 g (1 oz) cocoa
1 teaspoon lemon juice or vinegar
300 ml (½ pint) double or whipping cream
50 g (2 oz) plain chocolate, grated
few drops vanilla essence
225 g (8 oz) fresh strawberries, raspberries, or loganberries
icing sugar, for sprinkling

Prepration time: 15 minutes plus cooling
Cooking time: 2½-3 hours
Oven: 110°C, 225°F, Gas Mark ¼

The Pavlova is a dish of Australian origin, created in honour of the famous ballerina. The centre is slightly hollowed out and built up at the sides to suggest the dancer's tu-tu. Here it is adapted to make the best of English summer fruit.

1. Draw a 20 cm (8 inch) circle on non-stick silicone paper and place on a baking sheet.
2. Whisk the egg whites until standing in stiff peaks. Add 100 g (4 oz) caster sugar and whisk again until the mixture looks glossy and stands in stiff peaks.
3. Sift the cornflour and cocoa on to the meringue and fold in lightly but thoroughly together with the remaining caster sugar, and lemon juice or vinegar.
4. Spoon the meringue into the circle. Spread the meringue evenly, then slightly scoop out the centre and build up the meringue towards the edge of the circle.
5. Bake in a preheated oven for 2½-3 hours until the meringue is crisp on the outside and has a marshmallow texture on the inside. Carefully lift off the paper and cool on a wire tray. Ⓐ
6. Whip the cream. Fold the grated chocolate and vanilla essence into the cream and spoon into the centre of the meringue. Spread almost to the edge of the meringue and top with the fruit. Sprinkle with icing sugar just before serving. Once filled, the meringue is best eaten on the day it is made.

Ⓐ Can be made a day in advance and stored in an airtight container.

AUSTRIA

VIENNESE CHOCOLATE WHIRLS

Makes about 20
225 g (8 oz) butter or block margarine, softened, plus extra for greasing
50 g (2 oz) icing sugar
½ teaspoon vanilla essence
225 g (8 oz) plain flour
25 g (1 oz) drinking chocolate powder
50 g (2 oz) cornflour
To decorate:
100 g (4 oz) dipping or cooking chocolate
icing sugar, to dust

Preparation time: 20 minutes, plus cooling and setting
Cooking time: about 25 minutes
Oven: 180°C, 350°F, Gas Mark 4

1. Cream the butter and sugar together until light and fluffy. Add the vanilla essence and beat well.
2. Sift the flour, chocolate powder and cornflour over the mixture and whisk until smooth.
3. Fill a large piping bag fitted with a 2 cm (¾ inch) star nozzle and pipe 'S' shapes on to 2 greased baking sheets.
4. Bake in a preheated oven for about 25 minutes or until golden. Leave for 2-3 minutes, then lift on to a wire tray to cool.
5. Melt the chocolate in a small heatproof bowl set over a saucepan of hot water. Stir until smooth.
6. Dip half of each biscuit into the chocolate and cool until set on waxed paper or greaseproof paper.
7. Line up the biscuits with the chocolate ends in one direction. Cover the chocolate loosely with a sheet of greaseproof paper and dust the uncovered ends with icing sugar. Store in an airtight container for 2-3 days.

TOP: Chocolate pavlova BOTTOM: Viennese chocolate whirls

CARIBBEAN
CREOLE CAKE

Makes one 18 cm (7 inch) square cake
50 g (2 oz) dried apricots, finely chopped
4 tablespoons dark rum
50 g (2 oz) unsweetened desiccated coconut
1 tablespoon warm water
1 quantity Chocolate victoria sandwich mixture (page 51)
Fillings:
100 g (4 oz) plain chocolate, broken into pieces
15 g (½ oz) butter
25 g (1 oz) unsweetened desiccated coconut
1 tablespoon instant coffee powder or granules
1 tablespoon soft brown sugar
4 tablespoons boiling water
4 tablespoons apricot jam
300 ml (½ pint) double or whipping cream
Chocolate caraque (page 8), to decorate

Preparation time: 30 minutes, plus soaking
Cooking time: 25-30 minutes
Oven: 180°C, 350°F, Gas Mark 4

1. Soak the apricots in the rum for at least 4 hours.
2. Stir the coconut and water into the sandwich mixture and bake in two 18 cm (7 inch) square sandwich tins as directed on page 51. Turn out and cool, then cut one cake in half horizontally.
3. Place the chocolate and butter in a small heatproof bowl set over a pan of hot water until melted. Stir in the coconut.
4. In a second bowl, blend the coffee, sugar and water.
5. Finely crumble the uncut cake into a bowl. Spoon one-third into the rum and apricots, one-third into the chocolate and the remainder into the coffee syrup.
6. Spread one cut layer of cake with 2 tablespoons of the jam and place on a serving dish, jam side up. Spread over the rum and apricot mixture, making sure it is level, then the chocolate mixture and lastly the coffee mixture. Spread the remaining cake layer with the jam and press jam side down on to the layers. Ⓐ
7. Whip the cream and spread evenly over the cake. Decorate with chocolate curls.

Ⓐ Cover with cling film and chill overnight.

DENMARK

DANISH SPICE CAKE

Serves 8-10

225 g (8 oz) butter or block margarine
225 g (8 oz) caster sugar
275 g (10 oz) plain flour, sifted
25 g (1 oz) cocoa
2 teaspoons ground allspice
50 g (2 oz) plain or cooking chocolate
100 g (4 oz) chopped nuts (almonds, hazelnuts or walnuts), toasted
300 ml (½ pint) double or whipping cream

Preparation time: 20 minutes, plus cooling
Cooking time: about 18 minutes
Oven: 220°C, 425°F, Gas Mark 7

The dough for this cake is very fragile, and requires careful handling. It is best rolled out between sheets of greaseproof paper, as suggested in step 2.

LEFT TO RIGHT: Creole cake; Danish spice cake; English posset

1. Cream the butter or margarine and sugar until light and fluffy. Beat in the flour, cocoa and allspice until a smooth dough is formed. Divide into 6 equal pieces.
2. Place each piece between 2 sheets of greaseproof or non-stick silicone paper and roll out to a 20 cm (8 inch) diameter round, using a template or sandwich tin as a guide. Remove the top layer of paper and transfer each layer to a baking sheet. Prick all over with a fork. Bake in 3 batches of 2 baking sheets in a preheated oven for about 6 minutes, or until browned. Remove from the baking sheets but leave on the paper. If necessary trim the edges while still warm, then cool on a wire tray. Ⓐ
3. Melt the chocolate in a small heatproof bowl set over a pan of hot water. Stir until smooth, then spread the chocolate over the surface of one pastry disc and scatter over a quarter of the nuts.
4. Just before serving, whip the cream and combine the remaining nuts with the cream. Carefully peel the paper off the pastry discs and sandwich the layers together with the cream, ending with the coated disc, chocolate uppermost.

Ⓐ Can be made the day before. Keep in an airtight tin.

ENGLAND

ENGLISH POSSET

Serves 4-6

300 ml (½ pint) double cream, chilled
3 tablespoons drinking chocolate powder
1 tablespoon caster sugar
½ teaspoon ground cinnamon
2-3 tablespoons gin
50 g (2 oz) plain Chocolate scrolls (page 8)

Preparation time: 10 minutes, plus overnight chilling

The traditional English posset was a curdled drink, liberally laced with alcohol, sugar and spices, which was a delicacy as well as a remedy for colds. Here it has been turned into an interesting dessert which is especially nice with one tablespoon of the gin replaced with sloe or damson gin.

1. Pour the chilled cream into a chilled medium mixing bowl and whip until it just holds its shape on the whisk.
2. Add the chocolate powder, sugar and cinnamon and whisk in gently.
3. Whisk in the gin to taste, one tablespoon at a time, taking care not to overwhip the cream. If necessary, fold in the last tablespoon of gin with a metal spoon.
4. Spoon into tall glasses and top with the Chocolate scrolls. Chill overnight.

ENGLAND
CHOCOLATE BAKEWELL TART

Makes 12 slices
175 g (6 oz) plain flour
pinch of salt
40 g (1½ oz) butter or block margarine, chopped into
   pieces, plus extra for greasing
40 g (1½ oz) lard or white fat, chopped into pieces
1½ tablespoons water
Filling:
2-3 tablespoons raspberry jam
50 g (2 oz) butter or block margarine
50 g (2 oz) caster sugar
1 egg
50 g (2 oz) ground almonds
50 g (2 oz) cake crumbs
2 tablespoons cocoa, sifted
a little almond essence
25 g (1 oz) flaked almonds (optional)

Preparation time: 20 minutes
Cooking time: 25 minutes
Oven: 180°C, 350°F, Gas Mark 4

FRANCE
TRUFFLES

Makes about 20 truffles
1 teaspoon instant coffee powder or granules
1 tablespoon hot water
225 g (8 oz) plain chocolate, broken into pieces
75 g (3 oz) butter, cut into pieces
1 tablespoon top of the milk
2 tablespoons rum
1½ quantities crushed Praline (page 49)
75-100 g (3-4 oz) chocolate vermicelli

Preparation time: 25 minutes, plus cooling

These Truffles improve with standing so make them
2-3 days in advance and store in an airtight container.

1. Dissolve the coffee in the hot water. Place the coffee
and chocolate in a small heatproof bowl set over a pan
of hot water. Stir until the mixture is smooth and
thick.
2. Gradually add the butter, beating well between
each addition, then stir in the top of the milk, rum and
Praline. Cool in the bowl until firm, about 5-6 hours.
3. Divide the mixture into 20 equal pieces and roll
between the hands to form neat ball shapes.
4. Pour the vermicelli into a wide shallow dish or
plate and roll each truffle in them until completely
coated. Serve in paper cases. Keep cool.

1. Sift the flour and salt into a bowl, then rub the fats
into the flour until the mixture resembles fine breadcrumbs.
2. Add the cold water and mix with a round-bladed
knife then with the fingers to bind the dough into a
ball. Knead the pastry lightly on a floured surface. Ⓐ
3. Roll out the pastry and use to line a greased 18×
28 cm (7×11 inch) Swiss roll tin. Prick the pastry with
a fork. Spread the jam over the pastry.
4. Cream the butter or margarine and caster sugar
until light and fluffy. Beat in the egg. Fold in the
ground almonds, cake crumbs, cocoa and almond
essence to taste. Spread the mixture over the jam and
sprinkle with the flaked almonds.
5. Bake in a preheated oven for about 25 minutes. Cool
on a wire tray Ⓕ then cut into slices. It will keep for up
to 5 days in an airtight container.

Ⓐ Make the day before, cover and chill.
Ⓕ Thaw for 2 hours at room temperature.

LEFT TO RIGHT: Truffles; Chocolate bakewell tart; Finnish gâteau

FINLAND

FINNISH GÂTEAU

Makes one 20 cm (8 inch) gâteau
1 quantity Ganache torte sponge mixture (page 39)
2 tablespoons instant custard powder
2 tablespoons caster sugar
300 ml (½ pint) milk
250 ml (8 fl oz) sweetened apple purée
Icing:
175 g (6 oz) sugar
2 tablespoons cocoa
300 ml (½ pint) single cream
1½ tablespoons golden syrup
75 g (3 oz) butter, softened
25 g (1 oz) chopped almonds, toasted

Preparation time: 25 minutes, plus cooling
Cooking time: 30 minutes
Oven: 180°C, 350°F, Gas Mark 4

1. Prepare and cook the light cornflour sponge as for the Ganache torte (page 39) up to the end of step 3.
2. Blend the custard powder and sugar with a little of the cold milk and bring the remainder to the boil. Pour the boiling milk over the blended custard, stir well and return to the rinsed pan. Bring to the boil and cook for 2-3 minutes. Cover with damp greaseproof paper to prevent a skin forming. Cool.
3. When cold, beat the custard well. On a serving dish, sandwich the cake layers together with custard and apple purée, ending with a layer of cake.
4. Combine the sugar, cocoa, cream and syrup in a heavy based saucepan and stir over a low heat until the sugar has dissolved.
5. Bring to the boil, then boil gently until the mixture reaches 113-118°C, 235-245°F, on a sugar thermometer, or drop a small amount of the syrup into iced water. Mould the sticky syrup into a soft ball with the fingers. Remove the ball from the water. It should immediately lose its shape. Cool until soft and very thick.
6. Beat the butter gradually into the icing mixture.
7. Spread the icing over the gâteau and coat the sides with chopped almonds. This gâteau is best eaten on the day it is made.

FRANCE
BÛCHE DE NOEL

1 × 439 g (15½ oz) can sweetened chestnut purée
100 g (4 oz) unsalted butter, softened
225 g (8 oz) bitter or plain chocolate, broken into pieces
50 ml (2 fl oz) brandy or water
75 g (3 oz) caster sugar
1 teaspoon vanilla essence
To decorate:
2 glacé cherries
angelica
icing sugar

Preparation time: 15 minutes, plus chilling

1. Mash the purée in a mixing bowl until smooth, then beat in the butter.
2. Melt the chocolate with the water or brandy in a small heatproof bowl set over a saucepan of hot water. Stir vigorously until smooth, then gradually beat into the chestnut mixture.
3. Add the sugar and vanilla to the mixture and mix until thoroughly blended.
4. Line a 2 lb (1 kg) loaf tin with a large sheet of buttered greaseproof paper or foil, allowing plenty of overlap. Spoon the mixture into the tin and chill in the refrigerator until it begins to harden. Remove from the refrigerator and lift the paper or foil with the mixture out of the tin. Roll the paper or foil over the filling and work into a long round length to represent a log. Chill for at least 6 hours.
5. To serve, unwrap the log and place on a suitable serving dish. Draw a fork over the surface to roughen it and decorate with halved glacé cherries and strips of angelica. Keep chilled. Dust lightly with icing sugar just before serving.

LEFT TO RIGHT: Bûche de Noel; Colettes; Pacific gold

FRANCE
COLETTES

Makes about 15 cases

100 g (4 oz) plain, cooking or dipping chocolate, broken into pieces

Filling:
150 g (5 oz) plain chocolate, broken into pieces
1 teaspoon instant coffee powder or granules
1 tablespoon hot water
2 tablespoons single or double cream
50 g (2 oz) butter, cut into small pieces
2 egg yolks
1-2 tablespoons rum
crystallized violets, chopped, to decorate

Preparation time: 1 hour, plus setting and cooling

To keep the cases rigid, use a double layer of petit four paper cases or a single foil petit four case.

1. Melt the chocolate in a small heatproof bowl set over a saucepan of hot water. Stir until smooth.
2. One at a time, spoon a little chocolate into the petit four cases. With the tip of the little finger or a teaspoon, line the cases with half the chocolate.
3. When set, use the remaining melted chocolate to coat the chocolate cases again. Cool until firm.
4. To make the filling, melt the chocolate in a small heatproof bowl set over a pan of hot water. Add the coffee, dissolved in the hot water, and the cream. Stir until smooth and thick.
5. Away from the heat, gradually add the butter, beating well after each addition. When melted, beat in the egg yolks and rum. Leave until cool and thick, about 3-4 hours.
6. Carefully peel the paper or foil cases away from the chocolate and spoon, or pipe in the filling using a large star cake decorating nozzle. Decorate each colette with a piece of crystallized violet.

PACIFIC
PACIFIC GOLD

1 small to medium pineapple
½ quantity Brown bread and chocolate chip ice cream (page 13)
2 egg whites
100 g (4 oz) caster sugar
½ teaspoon vanilla essence

Preparation time: 30 minutes
Cooking time: about 3 minutes
Oven: 240°C, 475°F, Gas Mark 9

1. Carefully remove the top and bottom of the pineapple. Reserve the top and cut away any skin from around the leaves. Peel the pineapple and remove the eyes.
2. Cut the pineapple into about 4-6 slices and remove the core with a knife.
3. Beat the ice cream thoroughly, then sandwich 2 slices of pineapple together with the ice cream and fill the centre with more ice cream. Continue sandwiching the pineapple slices to make a 'whole' fruit.
4. Whisk the egg whites until very stiff, then add half the caster sugar. Continue whisking until the meringue is stiff and glossy, then fold in the remaining sugar and vanilla essence.
5. Fill a large piping bag fitted with a 2 cm (¾ inch) star nozzle and cover the pineapple with stars.
6. Bake in a preheated oven for about 3 minutes until the meringue points are tinged brown all over.
7. Remove from the oven and push the reserved leaves into position on top of the meringue pineapple. Serve immediately, or within 30 minutes after baking.

LEFT TO RIGHT: Russian cake; Celebration shortbread; Mazariner

RUSSIA

RUSSIAN CAKE

350 g (12 oz) Madeira cake
6 tablespoons sherry
a little red food colouring
5 tablespoons strawberry jam
icing sugar, for sprinkling
175 g (6 oz) marzipan
100 g (4 oz) plain chocolate, broken into pieces
15 g (½ oz) butter, plus extra for greasing

Preparation time: 20 minutes, plus overnight standing

1. Cut the Madeira cake into fingers.
2. Combine the sherry with a few drops of red food colouring.
3. Coat one side of each cake strip thinly, using 4 tablespoons of the strawberry jam, and layer in a greased 450 g (1 lb) loaf tin until half filled. Sprinkle with half the sherry mixture.
4. Continue layering until all the cake is used up. Sprinkle with the remaining sherry.
5. Lay a sheet of greaseproof paper on top and press the cake down well, then compress with heavy weights. Leave to stand overnight, then turn out on to a board.
6. Sprinkle a surface with icing sugar and roll out the marzipan into a rectangle that will completely cover the cake.
7. Brush the cake with the remaining jam and press on the marzipan. Trim if necessary.
8. Melt the chocolate in a heatproof bowl set over a saucepan of hot water. When smooth, beat in the butter and spread over the surface of the cake. Leave until set. Ⓐ
9. If liked, dust the top with icing sugar and serve cut into slices.

Ⓐ Store in an airtight container for 2-3 days.

MAZARINER

Makes about 12

2 quantities pastry from Chocolate cream pie recipe
   (page 28)
50 g (2 oz) butter
50 g (2 oz) caster sugar
1 egg
50 g (2 oz) ground almonds
few drops of almond essence
green food colouring
75-100 g (3-4 oz) dipping or cooking chocolate, broken into
   pieces
about 12 blanched almonds, toasted

Preparation time: 20 minutes
Cooking time: 15-20 minutes
Oven: 180°C, 350°F, Gas Mark 4

1. Roll out the pastry to about 5 mm (¼ inch) thick and use to line 12 deep tartlet patty tins. Prick the bases with a fork.
2. Cream the butter and sugar until light and fluffy, then beat in the egg. Carefully fold in the ground almonds, almond essence to taste and a few drops of green food colouring to make it pastel green.
3. Two-thirds fill each pastry case with the mixture, then bake in a preheated oven for about 15 minutes or until the filling is well risen. Cool on a wire tray.
4. Melt the chocolate in a small heatproof bowl set over a saucepan of hot water. Stir until smooth, then dip the top of each tart into the chocolate. Place an almond on each and cool until set.

CELEBRATION SHORTBREAD

Makes about 10 bars

100 g (4 oz) plain flour
50 g (2 oz) rice flour
100 g (4 oz) butter, plus extra for greasing
50 g (2 oz) caster sugar
50 g (2 oz) mixed chopped glacé fruits, washed and dried,
   e.g. cherries, angelica, pineapple
Topping:
40 g (1½ oz) butter
1½ tablespoons sugar
2 tablespoons milk
175 g (6 oz) icing sugar, sifted
2 tablespoons cocoa, sifted

Preparation time: 15 minutes, plus cooling and setting
Cooking time: 1¼-1½ hours
Oven: 140°C, 275°F, Gas Mark 1

1. Sift the flours into a mixing bowl and rub in the butter to the consistency of coarse breadcrumbs. Add the caster sugar and glacé fruits, then knead to a smooth dough.
2. Grease and line the base of an 18 cm (7 inch) square sandwich tin with greaseproof paper and lightly press the dough into the tin. Smooth over until level and prick with a fork.
3. Bake in a preheated oven for 1¼-1½ hours until the shortbread is pale golden brown. Stand for 10 minutes then carefully turn out, peel off the paper and cool on a wire tray.
4. When cold, return the shortbread to the sandwich tin. Melt the butter, sugar and milk over a gentle heat, bring to the boil, then pour over the icing sugar and cocoa in a mixing bowl. Beat until cool and stiff, then spread over the shortbread. Roughen the surface with a fork. When the topping has set, cut into bars.

SWITZERLAND

CHOCOLATE MUESLI SLICE

Makes 16 pieces
100 g (4 oz) clear honey
100 g (4 oz) butter or block margarine, plus extra for
   greasing
50-75 g (2-3 oz) soft brown sugar, to taste
225 g (8 oz) unsweetened muesli base
50 g (2 oz) sultanas
50 g (2 oz) hazelnuts, chopped
Topping (optional):
100 g (4 oz) plain chocolate, broken into pieces
25 g (1 oz) butter
1 tablespoon milk

**Preparation time: 10 minutes, plus cooling and
   setting**
Cooking time: 25-30 minutes
Oven: 180°C, 350°F, Gas Mark 4

If you wish to omit the topping, use 50 g (2 oz) of
chocolate drops for cooking in place of the sultanas.

1. Melt the honey, butter or margarine and sugar in a
saucepan. Stir in the muesli base, sultanas and hazelnuts. Mix well.
2. Line a 20×20 cm (8×8 inch) square sandwich tin
with greased greaseproof paper. Press the mixture
into the tin and spread evenly. Bake in a preheated
oven for 25-30 minutes until it begins to colour all
over. Take out of the oven and leave in tin. Cool
slightly.
3. Melt the chocolate in a small heatproof bowl set
over a pan of hot water. When smooth, beat in the
butter and milk. Pour the topping over the muesli
base and cool until almost set. Cut into 16 pieces and
leave in the tin until cold.

> Muesli was one of the best known items in the
> raw food diet devised by the Swiss Dr Bircher-
> Benner in the 1930s. He originally intended it to
> be rich in fruit – the modern version contains a
> lot more cereal. Although it is best known as a
> breakfast food, it makes a good meal at any time.
> Muesli base consists of a selection of cereals –
> rolled oats, cracked wheat, rye flakes, wheat-
> germ, bran, etc. – to which you add your own
> fresh or dried fruit and nuts. Muesli base can be
> bought in health food shops, delicatessens and
> some supermarkets.

U.S.A.

DEVIL'S FOOD CAKE

1 quantity Chocolate victoria sandwich mixture (page 51)
Syrup:
200 ml (8 fl oz) water
100 g (4 oz) brown sugar
2 tablespoons cocoa
4 tablespoons rum
Filling:
100 g (4 oz) plain chocolate, broken into pieces
2 tablespoons cream or top of the milk
few drops vanilla essence
1 egg, beaten
icing sugar, to dust

Preparation time: 25 minutes, plus soaking
Cooking time: 40 minutes
Oven: 180°C, 350°F, Gas Mark 4

Devil's Food Cake is a very rich chocolate cake almost
soft enough to eat with a spoon. It is sometimes made
with a white frosting, but here the delicious filling
and light dusting with icing sugar is ample.

1. Prepare and bake the Chocolate victoria sandwich
mixture in two 20 cm (8 inch) tins as directed on page
51. Turn out and cool on a wire tray.
2. Combine the syrup ingredients in a small saucepan
and heat gently until dissolved. Replace the cakes in
the tins. Make a few holes in the cakes with a fine
skewer and pour the syrup over them. Soak for 2-3
hours.
3. Place the chocolate in a small heatproof bowl set
over a pan of hot water. When melted, stir in the
cream or top of the milk, vanilla and egg. Stir
vigorously until smooth, then leave until cool.
4. When the filling is firm enough to spread, sandwich
the two cakes together with the filling and dust the top
with icing sugar.

For a decorative effect, place a patterned doily over
the top of the cake and dust with icing sugar. Carefully lift the doily away to reveal the pattern.

TOP: Devil's food cake BOTTOM: Chocolate muesli slice

INDEX